"Alli Patterson's contagious joy and ⸺ a trusted guide through Scripture to help you build a life—and faith—that can stand against anything. Honest about her failures and loving pursuit of God, Alli brings a fresh energy to your understanding of the Bible."

Lisa Harper, speaker, Bible teacher, and bestselling author of *Life 100 Day Devotional*

"I know few people who have more infectious joy about all things Bible as Alli. I'm thankful for her as my personal friend and as a gifted teacher with the ability to unpack both the theological and the practical sides of Scripture. Her insight will be a gift to any reader who picks this book up."

Brian Tome, founding and senior pastor of Crossroads Church, author, and host of *The Aggressive Life* podcast

"*How to Stay Standing* shows us how to build a life that matters, a life that endures even the roughest storms of life. Through vulnerable honesty and biblical truths, Patterson gives practical, actionable steps on how to build a rock-solid life by building our lives on Jesus. Building our lives on Jesus takes intentionality, but it is life changing and will help us stay standing no matter what comes our way."

Laura L. Smith, bestselling author of *Restore My Soul* and *How Sweet the Sound*

"I've been blessed to sit under Alli Patterson's teaching for the last fifteen years as her friend and fellow pastor at Crossroads. In *How to Stay Standing*, she shares her God-given gift for making a love of the Bible contagious and super practical. Read this book, and watch the God of the Bible come alive in a new way!"

Chuck Mingo, pastor and CEO of LivingUNDIVIDED and WorkingUNDIVIDED

"In *How to Stay Standing*, Alli Patterson shares powerful, personal insights and biblical wisdom to keep you standing firm in a fallen world. Her authenticity, understanding, and knowledge of the Word will forever change your life."

Richard and Brittni De La Mora, founders
of LoveAlwaysMinistries.com

"Faith seems the least likely thing to stand on. What if this substance is stronger than we think? Take a step of faith and read Alli's words. Then let's do what she teaches—come, hear, and practice."

Shauna Pilgreen, author of *Love Where You Live*

"If you are looking to be incredibly inspired—with very practical ways to connect with and enjoy God—this book is it. I found myself pausing, reflecting, and talking to God as I read her words. Alli has a way of writing that makes you stop and want MORE of God. My foundation is growing deeper and wider because of this book, and so will yours."

Amy Seiffert, speaker and author of *Starved*
and *Grace Looks Amazing on You*

"With refreshing honesty and authenticity, Alli Patterson leads us to bring every single part of who we are to Jesus, even when we're desperate, distracted, or doubtful. *How to Stay Standing* is a fresh, insightful, and practical guide to bringing your true self—all of who you are—into a vital, real relationship with the One who made you."

Dr. Alison Cook, psychologist and author
of *The Best of You* and *Boundaries for Your Soul*

"*How to Stay Standing* is a book we need right now. It's tempting to quit, sit, and wallow in our pain and disappointment, and for good reason. But we need to learn to get up again and not just live to fight another day but overcome the pervasive fear and sense of overwhelm in our culture. Alli teaches people to show up and tell the truth, to own their story and settle their soul, to expect resistance and grow in perseverance. She's a wise, funny teacher, and this book will bless you."

Ashley Abercrombie, author of *Rise of the Truth Teller* and *Love Is the Resistance*; cohost of the *Why Tho* podcast

"There's nothing like a life storm to make us realize how desperately we need a firm foundation. In the midst of swirling chaos, we long for something solid to stand on. Perhaps we intuitively know—in a Sunday school "fill in the blank" kind of way—that the answer to finding our footing in life is "Jesus," but often we still wonder "how?" In *How to Stay Standing*, Alli Patterson shares three practices that are doable yet deep. With her unique blend of clear biblical insight, relatable storytelling, and pastoral heart, she invites us to take her hand and join her on stable ground. Discipleship doesn't have to be fancy to be firm, and Alli charts a path which everyone everywhere can put into practice."

Bronwyn Lea, pastor and author of *Beyond Awkward Side Hugs*

HOW TO
STAY
STANDING

HOW TO STAY STANDING

3 Essential Practices for Building a Faith That Lasts

ALLI PATTERSON

Revell

a division of Baker Publishing Group
Grand Rapids, Michigan

Published by Revell
a division of Baker Publishing Group
PO Box 6287, Grand Rapids, MI 49516-6287
www.revellbooks.com

Printed in the United States of America

Library of Congress Cataloging-in-Publication Data
Names: Patterson, Alli, 1977– author.
Title: How to stay standing : 3 essential practices for building a faith that lasts / Alli Patterson.
Description: Grand Rapids, MI : Revell, a division of Baker Publishing Group, 2023.
Identifiers: LCCN 2022014419 | ISBN 9780800742836 (casebound) | ISBN 9780800742324 (paperback) | ISBN 9781493439881 (ebook)
Subjects: LCSH: Spiritual formation. | Jesus Christ—Example.
Classification: LCC BV4511 .P38 2023 | DDC 248.4—dc23/eng/20220720
LC record available at https://lccn.loc.gov/2022014419

Unless otherwise noted, Scripture quotations are from THE HOLY BIBLE, NEW INTERNATIONAL VERSION®, NIV® Copyright © 1973, 1978, 1984, 2011 by Biblica, Inc.® Used by permission. All rights reserved worldwide.

Scripture quotations labeled MSG are taken from *THE MESSAGE*, copyright © 1993, 2002, 2018 by Eugene H. Peterson. Used by permission of NavPress. All rights reserved. Represented by Tyndale House Publishers, Inc.

Scripture quotations labeled NASB are from the (NASB®) New American Standard Bible®, Copyright © 1960, 1971, 1977, 1995, 2020 by The Lockman Foundation. Used by permission. All rights reserved. www.lockman.org.

Scripture quotations labeled NET are from the NET Bible® copyright ©1996, 2019 by Biblical Studies Press, L.L.C. http://netbible.com. Scripture quoted by permission. All rights reserved.

The author is represented by Alive Literary Agency, www.aliveliterary.com.

Baker Publishing Group publications use paper produced from sustainable forestry practices and post-consumer waste whenever possible.

23   24   25   26   27   28   29   7   6   5   4   3   2   1

For Bill.
Thank you for your willingness
to discover together that Jesus was strong enough
to keep us standing. And thank you for always believing
in where God is taking me before I do.

CONTENTS

Part 3 **PRACTICE** **119**

INTRODUCTION

The Thing about Foundations

I always thought I was on solid ground, right up until my life collapsed.

I had cracks in the foundation of my life, and I really didn't see them. That's the thing about foundations: no one cares about them when everything's fine. They aren't sexy, and caring for them isn't the fun part of life, the highlight of your day, or the easy part of a relationship. Cracks in a foundation are silent and don't seem to matter for a long time. Until they do.

The house we live in now is built on a lot that slopes steeply downward in the backyard. When we put in an offer to buy this house, the paperwork indicated that the previous owner had built piers in the foundation. *Piering* is when steel support is placed below the existing concrete, and beams are driven through the old foundation to create greater support below. They stop the structure from moving when the ground around it shifts. Piers hold up what the old foundation no longer can.

This is exactly what God did to the foundation of my life. I had cracks that widened as the ground shifted. The support under me wasn't enough to hold up the life I wanted to build. I had built the framework of a great life by my early twenties—I just didn't have the foundation to hold it up. Worse yet, I didn't know it. God drove steel beams through me and into some stronger stuff below. If it sounds uncomfortable, it was. And it's also the reason I'm standing upright today.

Early on, I had a blueprint. I put my energy into building my "house," and I did it exactly the way I was "supposed" to. I learned how to build a life that was supposed to work: do well in school, be decent to other people, don't spend time in dark places. I knew how to work hard, commit to goals, and finish strong. I knew how to make and manage money. I knew how to be liked. I checked every box. I even found a great guy and we began to talk about how we'd build our life together. We both got high-performing careers and wanted to do some world travel. We focused on the house and not what it was standing on. And I especially liked the pretty parts of it.

The foundation of my life was, well, me. And it should have worked.

In some ways, my approach reminds me of the apostle Paul in the Bible. He was convinced he'd done life right. "I was advancing in Judaism beyond many of my own age among my people and was extremely zealous for the traditions of my fathers" (Gal. 1:14). Paul was a top-notch Jewish Pharisee trained by the best—faultless, according to the law and customs of Judaism. I, too, was voted "Most Likely to Succeed." Paul and I were set. We crushed life for a while, and we both found out later you can build strong but do it all on a bad foundation. Countless nice people have discovered the same.

The first signs that my foundation was crumbling appeared in college. I was distant from God. I began to notice patterns to the problems in my life—a ruthless focus on academic performance that created anxiety, a discomfort with communicating my own needs, a desire to keep things fine on the surface of relationships at the expense of being honest about my own thoughts and feelings. When the piers were put in our actual house, the homeowners hired a specialist—someone whose eyes were trained to see the sloped floor in the unfinished basement or the slightly twisted deck posts, someone who knew what that meant for the foundation of the house. But nope, I couldn't see those signs in my life at all. I wish I'd known to see them as warnings like the twisted deck or sloped basement. I was blinded by how solid everything looked. I guess my working theory was that if I was "good enough," I'd stay standing.

But as it turned out, I wasn't all that good.

Barely into my young marriage and professional career, I had an affair with a man at work. I was exactly what you'd think—a complete mess personally, professionally, emotionally, and relationally. I was too immature and too blind to see the cracks in my life that had led straight there. My husband and I had graduated, married, and moved to a new city within ten days and had no people there at all. I was seeking acceptance and approval at work and building my future on corporate success. This guy represented those things to me. At home we faced my husband's looming bar exam and then a dad diagnosed and lost to pancreatic cancer. We ignored the differences in our faith and often went to different churches or none at all. There was no emotional intimacy between us as we didn't know how to communicate what was in our hearts. We didn't know what emotional intimacy even was. We never learned to support each other in bad times because as yet we'd had only good times. A marriage is a life fully cultivated *together as one*. We weren't living as one, and I discovered really fast that I wasn't strong enough to hold it all up.

It was in my mess that I encountered a living Christ. He came to pier my foundation—not when I was strong but when I'd fallen into the gaping cracks. During this time, Jesus became the steel beam below me. It took a lot of support beams to get me standing again because I was already in a pile of rubble.

The first time I encountered Jesus face-to-face was in the middle of a run. Running had become my escape. I was running and crying and talking to him. I knew I couldn't live any real life in the tension of an affair. It was too dissonant. This life wasn't me; it was deceptive and disgusting. Except it *was* me. I felt trapped and didn't know how to get out. I knew the level of ruin I was looking at. Something stopped me right there on the sidewalk. I fell to my knees and said, "Get me out. However you need to. Break me."

Break me.

Those words had bounced around in my head for weeks. I knew they had been planted there by the Holy Spirit. I had a sense that they were serious, that I should not say them lightly. I knew they somehow signaled that I was ready for *his* plan and *his* way of busting in to come get me. Sounded scary. And ugly. And out of my control.

My first "yes" to Jesus in years was in those two little words.

Two weeks after I dared say them out loud, a chain of events went down that led to my confession. I went home one day and told my husband about the affair. The relationship was also exposed around that time at work. I knew God was behind it all. I knew the crash was coming before it came. I knew it when I said those words to God. As painful as it was, I had a strange certainty it was part of something that had to be done. And I was right. The old foundation just wasn't strong enough.

The weeks that followed were terrible. I felt more guilt, pain, hopelessness, and fear than I thought one person could take. I couldn't eat. The only peace I had was the split second as I opened my eyes each morning before my reality all came crashing down on me again. For months after, I wondered daily if my husband would even come home. I was a pariah at work. The "house" I thought I was building was in a heap at my feet.

But the God I encountered in that time changed my whole life. In my worst and weakest moment, I found something much,

much stronger, kinder, and better to stand on. I found the truth, compassion, and power of a living God who can hold up any life and rebuild after any fall. The first act of kindness was a vision I had one night while lying in bed. Alone. While I was wondering if "alone" would be my new normal, I felt God's arms around me. I saw a picture—sort of like a daydream—of two long, welcoming, strong, warm arms reaching down and encircling my entire home. Not just for me but for my husband, who was sleeping in the room next to mine. I felt warm and held and, for a moment, I knew he was there.

I caught another glimpse of this God in the mirror one day. I paused, studying my own reflection. I told her the ugly truth: "Alli, you're a liar, a terrible friend, a dishonest employee, and the worst wife." I stood looking in the mirror, sobbing at the truth of it all. But something else happened. Right there, in the painful truth of that confession, I also felt a rush of reassurance and relief that I didn't have to hold myself an inch above collapse anymore. I could let go and trust him instead of myself to hold it all together. I also felt his promise that one day I wouldn't even recognize this person I saw in the mirror. I knew deep down she wasn't me anyway.

I saw this amazing God *again* in a small room with the HR woman who I'd tried so hard to avoid. She was talking about what would happen to me at work—my reputation was another pile of rocks at my feet. I was crying; I couldn't look her in the eyes. She paused awkwardly and gently said, "Could I pray for you right now?" My head snapped up and my eyes got wide as the room filled with the presence of God. Even in my shame and heartbreak, Jesus got down underneath me to hold me up.

Every one of these moments was a beam driven into my crumbling foundation. Jesus took the time and care to convince me when I felt worthless that he is a God who does not agree. He showed me over and over that he meant his words: "Come to me, all you who are weary and burdened, and I will give you rest"

(Matt. 11:28). Jesus seemed to want me to come to him especially in the places where I wasn't on solid ground. It was in those spots he offered to let me stand on him.

He did that for the apostle Paul too. Paul had a huge collapse, but Jesus gave him a new foundation. You can read the story starting in Acts 9. Later, as Paul thought about the Jesus who chased him down with grace when he was at his worst, he recognized there was always a plan to rebuild his life. He wrote letters to the churches he planted about his own experiences with Jesus and how there was a plan in place for his life way before he knew it: "When God, who set me apart from my mother's womb and called me by his grace, was pleased to reveal his Son in me so that I might preach him among the Gentiles" (Gal. 1:15–16). God picked Paul even before his worst days, knowing they would come. God showed him the real Jesus so Paul could go on and tell others how to find this incredible strength and grace too.

It was during this time, the lowest time in *my* life, that I stumbled into the everyday habits of this book—coming broken to him, trying to read the Bible again, and risking actual moves of faith. Because I had nothing to lose, I told the truth to every question I was asked. I didn't have the energy to pretend anymore. It was obvious who I was, and it wasn't pretty. I confessed, apologized, took responsibility, and repented. I prayed every day—pretty much all day. I told God I was willing to follow him anywhere. And I really tried to do that. What I didn't know was that I was slowly uncovering the key of life as a disciple: *taking risks on God.* I risked telling the absolute truth and found forgiveness. I risked destroying the last bit of trust when I confessed and instead earned a tiny bit back. I risked a no when I asked, "Can you forgive me?" Instead, I heard a yes. Life as a Jesus-follower is full of all kinds of risks to convince us of the truth:

Everyone who comes to me and listens to my words and puts them into practice—I will show you what he is like: He is like a man building a house, who dug down deep, and laid the foundation on bedrock. (Luke 6:47–48 NET)

There's a life and a strength for you far beyond your own. There's a better foundation for your life than you or your money, your reputation, your connections, your adventures, your intelligence, or your morality and goodness. Paul and I and many others have preached the same gospel: Jesus died for your sins and rose from the dead according to the everlasting plans of God so that you could be offered a life that will never end, standing firm on the only foundation that's strong enough to last. And it's all by his grace. You will never deserve it. Whatever you build on him will stand. Nothing else will hold.

It's all about the foundation.

The good news is that no matter where you are when you start this book, Jesus can build or rebuild anything. He fills in cracks, adds steel beams, and drives piers through your old concrete. And you can meet him in three simple rhythms of faith.

Come to him. Hear his word. Practice it in your life.

Today is a day you either widen a crack or fill one in. Let's dig deep and build on rock.

1

LOOK DOWN

I'm not a big beach gal. When I get hot, I get cranky. I love the ocean view, but then I realize I'm just lying there sweating. I'll take the beach with a little hut, a fan, a cold drink, and a book. But I have four kids, so instead I get snack baggies, sand in my bathing suit, and sweat. I like to distract myself from the sweating by building sandcastles with the kids. Even as they get older, a couple of them still like to do it. The best spot to build them is just before the waves where the sand is packed and hard and still a little damp. We pat down bucket after bucket to build the three-tier castle. We dig moats and groom the roads with the little tool that looks like a minihoe.

And then the tide rolls in.

At first, one lone wave fills up the moats. That's fun, but fifteen minutes later, the waves erase the roads and start on the towers. At thirty minutes, the castle is nearly down, and little by little, the sand that was perfect for building is washed completely away by the changing shoreline.

When the kids were young, the crying would begin when the end became clear. They hated the thought of putting so much work into something that wasn't going to last. I would try to be sympathetic, but the truth was that it took everything in me not to say out loud what I was thinking: "Time for a science lesson, kids—the tide was predictable. It was always coming. You knew this was going to happen, or you could've if you'd thought about it. The castle was never going to last—especially not built right *there*!" (This is what I mean by "the heat makes me cranky.")

> As for everyone who comes to me and hears my words and puts them into practice, I will show you what they are like. They are like a man building a house, who dug down deep and laid the foundation on rock. When a flood came, the torrent struck that house but could not shake it, because it was well built. But the one who hears my words and does not put them into practice is like a man who built a house on the ground without a foundation. The moment the torrent struck that house, it collapsed and its destruction was complete. (Luke 6:47–49)

Jesus told this parable to a big crowd as the climactic finish to his famous sermon called the Sermon on the Mount. In this sermon, Jesus taught about living life as a disciple in his kingdom and finished by contrasting these two builders. Each was building a house, but one of them might as well have built a sandcastle. Jesus asked the crowd of listeners to look down and see what their lives were really standing on, what they were building life on top of. The material at the base of these two guys' houses was the only apparent difference—not the placement of the house, not the proximity to the water, not the possibility of encountering the flood. The only difference was what each house was standing on: one was on rock, one was not.

The rock was the key to survival when the water rose. You know very well that the water is going to rise—or at least you could if you let yourself think about it—the crippling anxiety you know is coming, the escalating power struggle with your boss, a decade of infertility, a school bully targeting your kid, the sudden need to care for an aging parent, the tragic overdose of a sibling, walking in to find another woman in your husband's bed . . . and that's just the people in *my* life! The water is rising over the roads in your life at this very moment. The tide is coming. Again. Jesus himself said it plainly: "In this world you will have trouble" (John 16:33). The apostle Peter added that we shouldn't even be surprised: "Dear friends, do not be surprised at the fiery ordeal that has come on you to test you, as though something strange were happening to you" (1 Pet. 4:12).

Even though trouble is inevitable, *collapse* is not. The rising waters will create instability in your life through trauma, transition, or turbulence. That's a guarantee. When they do, your foundation is either there or it's not. It's too late to dig for the rock then. You're either standing on it already or you aren't. In his parable, Jesus taught that anything but a life built on his Word will not stand. Even the best relationship, job, bank account, personality, or skill comes to a point where it just isn't strong enough to hold you up anymore. The time for digging for the rock is *before* the water rises. The time to look down is now. You don't want to build a sandcastle when the tide is rolling in.

> When the storm has swept by, the wicked are gone,
> but the righteous stand firm forever. (Prov. 10:25)

The head-scratcher for me when I read the parable of the wise and foolish builders (as it's commonly called) is that only one man in the parable seemed to realize trouble was coming—or we could at least say only one man truly acknowledged that reality with his actions. The man who saw trouble coming was the man who took the time to build his house well. He did what it took to dig, lay, and build on a foundation that could take a hit. The other guy didn't. He either didn't have the wisdom or didn't take the time and energy to dig for a foundation. Way too often, our first glance down to see if we're standing on something strong is when the trouble hits, and this is way too late.

When my husband and I got married, we didn't look down, and we were not building on rock. We didn't really think about what was down at the very bottom. We just knew we loved each other. We were both nice people. We both had educations to get jobs that could support us. We both wanted a family someday. We both hung the toilet paper the same way. We were set for better and only vaguely aware of the whole "for worse" idea. That theoretical trouble got real pretty quick. We moved to a new city immediately after the wedding and navigated the bumps of two new jobs, the stress of a bar exam, the reality of becoming real adults who pay bills, the trouble of making friends together, and, a short time later, the cancer diagnosis of my father-in-law. We had no idea how to communicate disappointments about each other and married life, but I still don't think we ever expected to completely collapse. We looked pretty darn solid. But the wisdom of the wise and foolish builders parable says that was exactly where we were always headed. The tide was always coming in.

When Jesus finished the Sermon on the Mount, he wanted his listeners to remember the big ideas, take them home, and live differently. Every great teacher knows the best way to drive home the main idea is with a great story. It sounds like Jesus chose a generic story about a theoretical storm to end this great sermon, but the parable was anything but generic. Jesus was way too good a teacher for that! Great teachers pick stories that are highly relevant to the lives of their listeners and dramatic enough to stick. As a teacher, I have never talked about floods, but I have told stories about a massive regional power outage, school shootings, and endless Zoom meetings during COVID lockdowns: shared experiences that my listeners immediately understood on many levels. Jesus told a parable about a flood because it was a shared experience. It was highly relevant to everyday life in Israel, and the cause of difficulty and decisions in the lives of everyone listening. It was through *this* kind of story that Jesus invited them to open up their eyes and look down at what they had built on.

As Jesus began the parable, right in front of his listeners' eyes was the Sea of Galilee. "They are like a man building a house, who dug down deep and laid the foundation on rock. When a flood came . . ." (Luke 6:48). They were standing on a large, flat-ish area at an elevation above the water, but they would have been staring right at the sandy shoreline of the sea with a bird's-eye view. The alluvial sand that made up the shore was a type that got very hard in the summer months, plenty hard enough to build something that would stand strong. However, the crowd would have known that wasn't the full story. They lived there all year long—not just in summer—so they knew something was coming that would change what they were looking at.

The Jordan River would be the reason for a huge change in the landscape: it's the major river through Israel even today. It starts near the northern border, then flows down through the middle of the country and into the Sea of Galilee where they were sitting. It

Shoreline of the Sea of Galilee

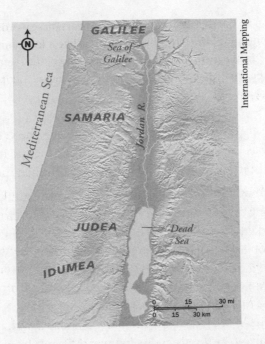

flows out again, continuing south until it empties into the Dead Sea. Along the way, the river branches into streams that were a main water source for most of Jesus's audience. The Jordan and its impact was everywhere in Israel. So, when the river flooded, it was a big deal.

In Israel, to ignore the reality of the Jordan floods was crazy: the floods happened every year. *Every* year. The rains *were* going to come. Predictably, the water was going to rise. Israel has always had fascinating patterns of winter and spring rains that come at highly predictable times. The crowd knew the danger of rising water and flash floods, exactly the type being described in the parable. The book of Matthew recounts this same parable with a more vivid description of the intense waters. It was serious.

The rain came down, the streams rose, and the winds blew and beat against that house; yet it did not fall, because it had its foun-

26

dation on the rock. But everyone who hears these words of mine and does not put them into practice is like a foolish man who built his house on sand. The rain came down, the streams rose, and the winds blew and beat against that house, and it fell with a great crash. (Matt. 7:25–27)

The sandy shoreline of the Sea of Galilee—the very spot the crowd was looking at—would have had great allure for many of Jesus's listeners. If you were a Galilean fisherman, building on the broad, strong, flat shoreline near the water meant big advantages for work and travel. But everyone knew that building there needed a different technique because anything built on the sand would go down in the floods. Not only fishermen were impacted by the floods. No matter where the crowds were from in Israel, Jesus's words still rang true: no one escaped the impact of the rains. For agricultural families, it would have been tempting to escape the heat of summer and build a house in a shady hollow carved out by the floods in previous years. People from mountain villages would have loved to build on the level banks by their Jordan-fed streams for ease of drinking water, feeding animals, cooking, and cleaning every day. For them, finding rock to build on meant hiking farther up the hillside, taking significantly more time and effort for daily life. No matter what geography in Israel, building without putting in the extra care or effort to find rock for a foundation would have been so much easier. But they also knew what would follow when the rains came.

This is exactly what Jesus wanted every ear in the crowd to walk away understanding: the consequences for choosing speed or comfort or convenience in their own lives were exactly the same. It's always easier to pretend like it will always be summer.

The parable challenged the crowd to look beyond a midsummer view of their lives. It was an invitation to a life that would stand for all eternity. Building for *now*, for convenience or for speed—well, that was as crazy as forgetting where you lived! It would be like living in Israel and pretending the Jordan wasn't going to flood! Instead, Jesus wanted them to build a life and a faith *on him*. And all it would take? Actually putting his words into practice.

I like to stick my head in the summer sand every now and then, though. I found proverbial sand in my hair one Tuesday night when I flopped down on my bed and groaned to my husband, "I don't want to talk to him. I'm exhausted. I want to just let this go . . . but I don't think we can." While changing bedsheets I'd discovered that my son had been hiding a laptop in the space between his bed and his wall. When I looked at it, I discovered he'd been watching stuff late at night. No, it wasn't porn. The content actually wasn't a problem, but we have a rule: all devices come out of the bedrooms and charge in the study overnight. It's crystal clear. He'd definitely heard those words. And he'd chosen not to practice them.

Ugh. We'd *just* been through some other character development stuff with this same kid. We'd *just* been the parents who'd "made a big deal" about some stuff lately. I didn't want to be *that* mom again. I didn't want to have another awkward conversation and watch him feel bad. I laid there wishing I'd never tried to be nice and change his stupid sheets. I just wanted to go to bed. No one has the energy for this at 10:42 p.m. on a Tuesday. I didn't want to dig through the hard sand; I wanted to go only far enough to put my head in it.

But this is the moment you decide: Are you digging to the rock or not? I know very well the storms that are coming in my son's life. I know he's going to face rules he doesn't agree with again. I know he'll have bosses he doesn't like. I know he will think he knows better. And I also know he will need real integrity to get through situations just like this. He'll need rock under his feet.

It's never hard to find a reason to look the other way. It's never hard to choose easier, faster, less conflict. But ten thousand Tuesday nights are how you dig down to the rock. They're the hard work of foundation-building. And quality takes longer to build.

For no one can lay any foundation other than the one already laid, which is Jesus Christ. If anyone builds on this foundation using gold, silver, costly stones, wood, hay or straw, their work will be shown for what it is, because the Day will bring it to light. It will be revealed with fire, and the fire will test the quality of each person's work. (1 Cor. 3:11–13)

It's only when the storm comes that you see whether a foundation got laid. The wise only look wise when the water is rising and they're still standing. If you really have built on the rock, the flood doesn't pull you under.

Just a few years ago when I fell down a big flight of hardwood stairs, I broke my rib and punctured my lung. It was a moment when I had cause to look down and notice some rock beneath my feet. We had lived in our community for over twenty years at that point. We had tried to be faithful friends, but we are a normal family and life gets crazy. I rarely looked down: I hadn't thought about how long we'd truly been building community with all those Tuesday nights. It was rock, forming right under my feet. The night the flood came in, I ended up in the hospital. I was hurting. I couldn't build those friendships in the emergency room. At that point we either have them or we don't. Our community was the only reason life worked for a while—driving when I couldn't; cleaning when I couldn't; helping me mother my kids; decorating my house for holidays; knowing me well enough to leave me a bag of Blow Pops on my porch when I was in pain. My life flooded because, well, crap happens. But I didn't collapse.

To my son on the night we found the laptop, it looked like we were doing things "the hard way" or "making a big deal about things" into which others don't put as much time or effort or boundaries. If you dig down to the rock when the weather is decent, you might just look a little over-the-top. I would have loved to just say "he's a good kid" and gone to bed. Every single time we choose to dig down deep when our circumstances are still dry and sunny on the surface is another inch toward the rock. The payoff might not come for years. We busted him out on a Tuesday night and dealt with it because we knew the flood was coming. We want him to be a man of integrity. We want him to respect authority. We want him to be able to articulate thoughtful objections instead of sneaking around. We want him to experience the truth that when you break rules, you—by default—choose a set of consequences. When the water rises is when you—and everyone else—find out whether it was really rock you were standing on.

The difference between lives that stand and lives that fall is only the foundation. In this parable Jesus audaciously claimed to be the rock below the sand for every life. He is the cornerstone, the strongest, first, and most important rock of whatever you are building. If the cornerstone is missing, defective, or not laid properly, the whole building is off. In Isaiah 28:16, God spoke about laying a foundation with a cornerstone strong enough to build *eternal* lives on:

> So this is what the Sovereign LORD says:
> "See, I lay a stone in Zion, a tested stone,
> > a precious cornerstone for a sure foundation;
> the one who relies on it
> > will never be stricken with panic."

The apostle Peter quoted that passage as he wrote about Jesus and called him out as the cornerstone prophesied by Isaiah: the "living stone rejected by men but chosen and precious in God's sight" (1 Pet. 2:4 NET). Jesus is the only sure foundation. A life standing on him requires looking beyond summer to see that life extends far beyond here and now; it also requires knowing that here and now is the time to dig for the rock.

Not all of us are up for it. Jesus knew that too. It's why he spoke this parable to this particular audience. Jesus was talking to people exactly like you: people who had come to hear him *on purpose.* They weren't eye-rollers or scoffers; they nodded in agreement as he spoke of generosity, prayer, fasting, not worrying, and not judging others. Like you, most of them were "nice people" who agreed with things like that. Jesus told that parable *to believers*, to people who called him "Lord." The nicer you are, the greater the potential for this particular blind spot in your faith. Jesus said to the crowd just before this parable, "Why do you call me 'Lord, Lord' and do not do what I say?" (Luke 6:46).

Nice people rarely see the crash coming. The parable of the wise and foolish builders is Jesus's warning to nice people everywhere. The self-deception Jesus warned about was saying you have faith while not actually doing what he commanded his followers to do. After spending time teaching and instructing thousands of people on how to live as his followers, he ended with this parable, essentially saying, "Not all of you are real followers. You think you are, but you're not." We'd all be lying if we said we haven't sometimes been the one who nods along and then pauses the podcast or leaves church and continues life just the way we were already living it. None of us are as nice as we think we are. Jesus said any of us can become real followers if, like the crowd that day, we hear his words and actually put them into practice in our lives. Everyone else is self-deceived and headed for a crash. Ouch, Jesus. This parable is a challenge to actually DO something, to have your faith laid bare when the water rises and be standing in the end.

> As for everyone who comes to me and hears my words and puts them into practice, I will show you what they are like. They are like a man building a house, who dug down deep and laid the foundation on rock. When a flood came, the torrent struck that house but could not shake it, because it was well built. But the one who hears my words and does not put them into practice is like a man who built a house on the ground without a foundation.

The moment the torrent struck that house, it collapsed and its destruction was complete. (Luke 6:47–49)

Sometimes the main point in the parables of Jesus is really confusing, but not this one. The meaning is obvious: Jesus is inviting you to actually obey his teaching, and in doing so, put your life on the only foundation that will stand for all eternity. Jesus can be the rock of your life, but you'll have to actually do what he says. But the good news is that—right there in plain sight with the parable—he gave you the way there. In one sentence Jesus revealed a simple pattern for how to ground your life on him: "As for everyone who comes to me and hears my words and puts them into practice, I will show you what they are like" (Luke 6:47).

Come to me.

Hear my words.

Put them into practice.

A faith built through the continual rhythms of *come, hear,* and *practice* will put you on the rock and will build you what lasts. Lives of lasting faith always have evidence of these three simple but profound practices. We are going to explore them in depth together. These three practices are how you dig for the rock. They're going to take you from a listener in the crowd *around* Jesus to someone who is standing *on* Jesus.

First, we **come**. To come is not just to put ourselves in the proximity of Jesus, but to actually come before him with an open willingness to engage. When Jesus said "come," he didn't mean physically; he meant to bring our whole heart, self, and life before him. So—with our real stuff—come to him.

The second practice is **hear**. When we let the Word regularly into our lives, we begin to know God so much more—his language, history, character, tone of voice, and his very words through the pages of the Bible. Hearing is more than physical listening. Hearing sinks deeper and impacts what we are willing to do. Which lands us right at the third rhythm of **practice**.

When we come with our hearts open to hear and we hear deeply enough that it moves us to practice real obedience in our lives, it's only then that the rock is formed at our feet. In the parable, the foolish builder is likened to a man who never put the words he heard into practice. A life of faith in the words of Christ will always compel us to the action of risky, heartfelt obedience. Practice is what finishes the process of turning the sand of our foundations into rock. We'll be *grounded* on Jesus himself. We all have some words of Jesus that we need to move on, so we're going to practice together.

The Jordan is going to flood. Sooner or later, you'll find out what's under your life, but you don't have to wait to look down. Don't stick your head in the sand. Come. Hear. Practice real faith. In no time at all, waves that would have crushed you before . . . won't. Jesus invited you to look down and dig for an eternal life through *come, hear, practice*. There's no reason you can't start today; tomorrow the ground under your feet will feel a little firmer.

I saw the little red light blinking as I walked by. The only reason I stopped at the guest bedroom that day was to push the button on the answering machine. I listened as my mother-in-law finished her voice message like a letter. Just as I heard, "Love, Mom," I glanced down at the old wood Home Depot cube that was still holding some random books from its former days as my college nightstand. I noticed my old Bible with a green pleather cover. For some reason, I reached down; it had been in the same spot for so long the fake leather stuck to the inside of the cube as I tugged it out. I laid down across the bed, propped myself up on one elbow, and opened it. All I remembered of the Bible was the four names of the Gospels and that the red words were Jesus talking. I reread the handwritten note across the title page from my childhood best friend Amy. She had given me this Bible in our late teen years—maybe for a birthday or my graduation. It was inscribed in gold on the front cover with my maiden name, Alli Simpkins. I ended up using that same Bible for years to come—so long that my coworkers in my first ministry job used to call it the "Alli Simpkins Bible." But that day when I found it again, I was coming to it for the first time in a long time. Things were not very good. My marriage was distant and in recovery. I'd burned a lot of bridges. I needed a friend. Jesus used to feel like one years before that; maybe that was why I picked up the Bible that day. Was Jesus still around? How could I find him if he was?

For reasons unknown, I said to Jesus in the guest room that day, "I'm here. Are you still here? Will your words help me?" I hadn't come to him in so long that I forgot what it felt like to hear his voice, so I wasn't surprised at the silence in return. I felt a little sad as I flipped through, realizing whatever I used to know of it was gone. But as I laid there in our old-stuff-from-college room, I was genuinely open. Hoping. Willing. I had no idea that's all he really wanted, that I'd already begun the digging that was going to lay a new foundation.

"Come to me" is Jesus's invitation. In the parable of the wise and foolish builders, Jesus said, "As for everyone who comes to me and hears my words and puts them into practice, I will show you what they are like. They are like a man building a house, who dug down deep and laid the foundation on rock" (Luke 6:47–48).

Coming to Jesus is the very first rhythm of building a faith that lasts. Sometimes Christians talk about when they came to Jesus, meaning the point in time when they first understood the gospel and received the forgiveness for sin and new life available in Christ. That is a huge moment of coming to him, but it is really just the beginning of a lifetime of coming back again and again. Coming to Jesus isn't a one-time deal; it's the ongoing, regular practice of bringing yourself before him, open and ready to take whatever he might have to give. Jesus spoke this invitation into a huge crowd on the day he shared that parable. It was a crowd seated on the grass and large rocks around him, listening to his teaching. This begs the question: Hadn't they already come? The people he said this to were sitting right there, surrounding him.

Jesus could have only meant that coming wasn't primarily a physical act but something else altogether.

I'm sure you've been in meetings at work or in classes at school where people talk about things. In those kinds of meetings, I multitask. I keep one ear open while answering my emails on my phone. I've come, but barely. Jesus drew that same line with his words to that crowd. He made a distinction between being physically present and being open and willing to engage wholeheartedly. The crowd around Jesus was present, but most of them hadn't yet come to him. He was after much more than sitting there with a head nod of interest while the crowd went about other things. He was looking for people who said, "Here's all of me. So where do we go from here?" When Jesus gave the Sermon on the Mount that day, he invited everyone, even though he knew not everyone would be willing. The second builder in his parable did not come. That guy started with only hearing the words. It was as if he was sitting there but was engrossed in checking his email. It does not go well for that guy in the parable. To stay standing, it requires the depths of the heart.

> As for everyone who **comes to me** and hears my words and puts them into practice, I will show you what they are like. They are like a man building a house, who dug down deep and laid the foundation on rock. When a flood came, the torrent struck that house but could not shake it, because it was well built. But the one who hears my words and does not put them into practice is like a man who built a house on the ground without a foundation. The moment the torrent struck that house, it collapsed and its destruction was complete. (vv. 47–49, emphasis mine)

To come is to bring the fullness of yourself—not just your body, but your heart and soul and mind as well. This was not an idea that started with Jesus's life on earth. God had been telling his people that he wanted their hearts from the beginning.

This is shown in the traditional daily prayer in ancient Hebrew culture called the Shema in Deuteronomy 6:4–5: "Hear, O Israel: The LORD our God, the LORD is one. Love the LORD your God with all your heart and with all your soul and with all your strength." It was this idea that Jesus meant when he said, "Come to me." He meant bring it all.

"Come" is not just an invitation; it's also a command. Jesus repeated these words in Mark 12 when he was asked by a teacher of the law to confirm which was the greatest commandment. He answered with "Love the Lord your God with all your heart and with all your soul and with all your mind and with all your strength" (v. 30). If you want to find and follow Jesus, his command is to come and bring it all. "Come" is the one-word command Jesus issued to multiple people in the Scriptures who wanted to become his disciples. The implications of this word carry the hint of a challenge. If you want to be a follower of Jesus, I think he'd say, "Great. I'll take your whole self and nothing less."

The day Jesus told the parable of the wise and foolish builders, he implied that just sitting on nearby rocks wasn't enough. As you know if you've ever been dragged to church by someone, being in a place where people talk about Jesus is not the same as coming to him yourself. The Bible contains a lot of religious types who spent their whole lives trying to get close to God in a church-like setting, keeping church-like rules, and then completely missing Jesus right in front of their own eyes. You could spend years being in the crowd at a spiritual place and never live a life grounded on Jesus. I'm pro going to church because many of them are environments that open our hearts and minds to God. I've certainly come to Jesus during a church service, but it happens much more often in my everyday life. Coming is personal. It's between you and him. It's entirely about the position of your heart and your willingness to dig deep for an authentic exchange with a living God.

When I think about the moments I have truly come to Jesus, they're wildly different—all over the map. Sometimes I'm sad.

Sometimes it's a Wednesday at 6:15 a.m. with my favorite coffee mug in hand. Sometimes I'm standing in awe of something he created. Sometimes I have had a question or an idea that I just can't get rid of, and I finally ask him about it. Sometimes I'm singing words in my car at the top of my lungs on the highway in response to him. Sometimes I'm discouraged or rejected. Sometimes I'm desperate or trapped at a dead end of my own bad choices. Sometimes I'm literally on my knees. Whatever the emotion or life scenario, they all have one thing in common: I'm ready to hear what Jesus has to say. And I just tell him that.

Sometimes coming to him sounds like, "Good morning. I'm here to be with you." Sometimes it's a frustrated, "Where do I go now?" Sometimes it's a little giggle of joy at an inside joke between us. Sometimes it's a weary, "What do I do with this?" Or an angry, "Say something!" Or a wordless sigh. Or a pent-up feeling of finally giving words to something I was resisting admitting out loud. When I genuinely come, I open myself up to the idea that Jesus has something for me in that place. And I also have to risk that he'll stay silent.

I've caught myself staying away from him because of this risk: I'm afraid I'll open myself up and come and there will just be . . . crickets. Other times I've held Jesus at arm's length because I knew what his words said about something, and I didn't want to hear it. Sometimes I don't come to him because I just forget I can. Sometimes it's because I'm afraid he'll be mad at me or be mean to me. Sometimes I stay away because I am not done trying to do it my way.

I tried the "avoid Jesus" approach until the day I threw myself down on the leather love seat in my bedroom. I had taken a new and significant leadership role on staff at the church. I took it because I was a good leader. I took it because I was asked. It had only been about four weeks since I'd started when I had a dream about being way up high on a very rickety platform. I had awakened to a sense that something was very wrong with the job. In the few weeks that followed, I had another dream about it and a growing sense that I needed to get out of this job. I couldn't shake the thought. I couldn't escape the urgency. I tried every which way in my mind to justify staying in it. Who leaves a job they just got? How bad does *that* look? When I threw myself onto the love seat that day, it was me coming to Jesus. I hadn't been ready before that. I hadn't been open to all possibilities, and I knew it. But that day I came. I was ready to figure out what in the world I was going to do. I was ready to admit that I'd potentially made a mistake. I was ready to ask questions, and I was open to the answers. I came out of my resistance and avoidance and came to Jesus instead. I was finally over the voice in my head that said, "Give it a while and see if it gets better." I came to Jesus saying, "Okay, okay, I give up. I'm here. Where do we go from here?"

We all have doubts about whether God's going to be there. We all have fears about what he might ask us to do. We all have weird baggage from our preconceived notions of what it means to live a life following him. Whatever your halfways and hang-ups, bring them along. Don't let them stop you from coming. A word of warning: there's no faking this. And this isn't a performance for anyone else. God knows if you're all there or if you're holding something back from him. To come is an internal, invisible reality, but it's a reality nonetheless. If you want a foundation of faith that lasts, it has to be with a God who can handle the real you. That's exactly who you'll find waiting for you when you show up. So, come.

Show up.

Tell the truth.

Kneel down.

That's how you come.

2

SHOW UP

On my wedding day, I was more and more overwhelmed with every step. I scanned the faces on both sides of the aisle, and all I kept thinking was, *I can't believe they all came*—my best friend's parents, my husband's high school basketball coach who was the catalyst to our second date, my college roommates, my favorite cousin from Kansas, longtime neighbors from my childhood, my grandparents. Every person I had loved over the course of my whole life was in one place. There's a lot I remember about my wedding day, but very few memories are stronger than the memory of the feeling I had as I walked down the aisle taking in all the faces. They weren't names on RSVP cards anymore. They were real people right in front of me. I was overwhelmed with love.

As I reflect back on what it was about this particular moment that moved me, it was not just seeing everyone in one place at one time; it was the cost. Each person had paid a significant price to be there—in weekend plans, in babysitters, in gifts, in gas or hotel rooms, not to mention the emotional investment closer friends and family made to support me. The collective price they'd paid to come and be with me was overwhelming. I felt a deep sense of my own value because of their presence. Presence is love because presence is sacrifice. When you show up somewhere, you've paid for it with your time, sometimes your money, and definitely with the nos you've said to other people and plans you could've had. Over twenty years later I still feel the impact of that collective act of love. They came.

One of the upsides for me during the COVID-lockdown era was the relief of *not* having to show up for things. I actually painted my bedroom with the camera off on Zoom calls; it was glorious. It can be a huge relief when you don't have to fully show up. It just requires so much less of you. I know I'm not the only one who's been relieved at an occasional night-out cancellation so I could stay in my pj's and do laundry. But COVID was like a fast-paced sociological experiment—a year later we were all living the downside of never showing up. My relationships suffered because we were never *together*, face-to-face, making it impossible to have the benefits of coming into each other's presence.

Our connection to Jesus operates the same way. If you want a life that feels connected to God and grounded on Christ, you're going to have to show up. And showing up is going to cost you something. To show up for someone, you've got to know where and when you're meeting. You need a regular cadence of being together. Yes, of course, there are also spontaneous meetups and quick connections—those are sometimes very sweet moments. But without a regular time and place, you won't establish the strength the relationship really needs. The benefits of showing up for each other just won't be there.

You need to define a time and a place to come and be present with Jesus.

Don't tell me you talk to Jesus on the go. I hope you do! But that's not going to get you down to a foundation of rock. My mom once asked me why I don't text my brothers more often. I love my brothers, but they are both far away, and at best I see them physically once a year and sometimes much less. I realized we don't text much because we don't have an ongoing, connected relationship. Texting adds color and timely connection to a friendship, but there's a reason why you text your *best* friend the most! You've built the strongest foundation, and with that comes the luxury of also talking in abbreviations and emojis. You don't do that with long-lost relatives because they don't get your tone, your unique language, and your day-to-day life. I love a good "help me find a parking spot" prayer at Target, but that's not enough to stand with Jesus. You need regular connection.

I show up as fully as I can during my first hour of the day (okay, it's almost always at least thirty minutes). Your time doesn't have to be the early morning, but this particular hour of the day is the most consistent for me. It was a struggle to offer this time to God. For a long time, I'd resisted showing up in that specific time and place. Mostly it was because I hate showering twice in one day. I know how silly that sounds. But I like to do things efficiently, so if I just work out first thing in the morning, then I won't have to get sweaty later on and clean myself up again. Makes perfect sense, no?! For years I ran or worked out first thing in the morning because that's how I liked it, because that's how my day worked best. As I began to hunger for a stronger connection with God, I tried all kinds of other times to meet—lunch, right before bed. I'd even convinced myself for a while that I could do it *while* I ran. All these moments are certainly times I can connect with Jesus, but they are lacking the consistency or the intentionality it takes to really show up. Slowly I realized what I needed to do, and then I acted like a brat about it. *But, God! What about my runs? The first hour of the day is mine!*

It took me longer than it should have to make time to show up because of my tight grip on this part of my day. I was holding on to it because I was afraid if I gave it to Jesus, it wouldn't be good for me. *If I give up this workout time, what if I can't find time later? If I can't work out exactly the way I want to, will I start gaining weight?* Ugh! There they were, age-old body image issues. I realized I was planning my schedule around managing them. Sounds like something I needed to take to Jesus. I'm sure you have your reasons, too, about why you can't meet on the regular—you're not a morning person or you're not disciplined enough or you work too hard or you have too many kids. I get it. I've said them all too.

At first, I experimented with one day per week. I met with Jesus instead of going to the gym on Wednesday mornings. I worked my way up to the commitment I now hold: at least five days per week, nothing comes before starting my day with him. No matter when or where you show up, you'll certainly receive no judgment from me; I've been there. But make no mistake, **if you want to be able to find and follow Jesus, then you will have to define a time and place to show up and be with him**. There is wisdom you want and truth you need that you won't have access to any other way.

> All things have been committed to me by my Father. No one knows the Son except the Father, and no one knows the Father except the Son and those to whom the Son chooses to reveal him.
> **Come to me**, all you who are weary and burdened. (Matt. 11:27–28, emphasis mine)

Come to Jesus. Show up to be with him because he knows all things, because he can reveal the heart of God to you, because he wants to deal with your burdens. *In him* all the treasures of wisdom and knowledge that you need are hidden, but it takes some time, some quiet, and some intentionality to dig them up. My husband says, "Five minutes is better than zero minutes." Start anywhere, but start showing up regularly.

Whatever time and place you pick doesn't have to be forever. *Think seasonally.* Define a time and place you can keep to for a short season—maybe just one to three months. It doesn't *have* to be the morning, but at least consider it because of the obvious way it grounds your day and your heart for what's ahead.

I've got ten questions to ask yourself that will help you get to a regular time and place. They're not complicated to ask, but they can be hard to answer because they require actual decision-making. Get ready! Start with only considering the next month. If it's summer and you can do it outside at a park, great! Don't worry about winter yet. If your kids sleep late when it's dark out so you'll have a little extra time this month, great! Do that. Don't try to define a long-standing pattern. Just start for a short season. Go get your calendar and answer the first four questions:

1. What day(s) of the week can I arrange time to myself?
2. What time(s) of the day could I get at least twenty uninterrupted minutes?
3. What is the place I will be in?
4. How long can I commit to keeping this time/place?

I even have a chair. It's a blue chair in my living room. In the summer, I move to the leather chair in the study because people are getting up at different times. During the darker months of the year, I always light a candle. I get my coffee, my Bible, and my notebook. I leave my phone somewhere else. You don't have to do it like me. You might want to be outside. You might not want to write down a word. You might need to be somewhere you can talk out loud. Whatever! Just come for a season, and then change your answers to the questions above if you need to.

The one thing I don't want you to do is make the mistake of thinking it'll be easy to keep this time. You're going to have to fight for it because there will likely be a cost. Let's consider the cost right now. What will this cost you? An awkward conversation with your roommate? A request for help from your spouse? The money for a babysitter? A regular time at the gym? Whatever it is—pay it. Or ask God for the help you need to be able to pay it. What you get back will be worth so much more! Show up to be with Jesus, and arrange everything else around that time. Next, ask yourself:

5. What will this cost me?

Life gets upside down, and sometimes you just can't make a regular time. I get it. When I had newborns, I beat myself up terribly for not being able to keep to a regular time and place. I had four of them in a six-year period, so I beat myself up off and on for over half a decade. Don't do that. God had so much more grace for me than I had for myself in that season. I was up around the clock, had toddlers pulling at me all day, and couldn't even manage to shower some days. I remember a friend who told me I should be sitting on the couch with my Bible during every nap time, and I wanted to punch her in the face. What about returning a phone call to a friend, taking a bath, or just sitting in blissful silence?

This is exactly why I say think seasonally. There are seasons when you have to be creative or only have the possibility of an on-the-go connection with Jesus. These short seasons are exactly why you need a regular time and place right now. Just like your best friend who completely understands when you disappear for a few weeks due to a big project at work, Jesus gets it too. There's grace for you. As the season ends, just start fresh. Showing up now means your relationship will be ready for the brief times when you just can't.

Showing up is not a small thing. When you come to Jesus by physically showing up, there are going to be issues. Sometimes our hearts and intentions are good and we're up for it but then the distractions hit! I've picked up my phone to look up a Bible verse, and ten minutes later found myself mindlessly scrolling Instagram. Some are regular old external distractions like your phone, a kid waking up early, or the toilet overflowing. I always seem to think of things to add to my to-do list as soon as I sit down! Now I try not to be fooled. As soon as I get my phone in my hand or my booty out of the chair, I'm done. It's over. So if you want to show up, you need to add these questions to the list:

6. What are common external distractions for me? (Your phone needs to be on this list.)
7. What can I do to deal with these ahead of time?

My friend Elizabeth and I used to get together every New Year's Eve with our families. Three NYEs in a row ended with a trip to urgent care that killed the rest of the evening. By the third one, we were forming conspiracy theories about why our families were being kept from ringing in the new year together. Don't be surprised if your attempts to show up feel like someone is conspiring against the time and place you pick. Don't be surprised if it falls apart a few times, especially early on. Don't be surprised if you cannot think of anything other than the crumbs on the floor by your chair. You might come and feel like your time was fruitless. Not every time will be magical; you are digging down through the dirt and looking for the rock, not floating on clouds. Not one time that you show up to be with Jesus is worthless to him: keep pushing through distraction. The world, your flesh, and the enemy of God are all against you showing up. Any time in your life that has the potential to produce a closer connection with God is going to be opposed. When you show up repeatedly, the distractions will lessen. Keep showing up.

Maybe you just aren't fully on board with rearranging stuff in your life to show up and spend time with Jesus. You're either not sure of him or not convinced he's worth the trouble and cost. Truth be told, right now you're probably not going to do it because you just don't really want to. Or you're afraid or annoyed about what it might mean for you. Or you just don't feel like you need it.

Yet.

A guy named Paul was much further away than wherever you are right now. Well, for this story, his name was still Saul. (He was referred to as Paul after Jesus changed his heart. For the beginning of his story, see Acts 9–13.) Saul was alive at the same time as Jesus and was a top-notch Jewish Pharisee. He was admired and clearly thought he had life figured out. He knew the law, observed it carefully, and felt his life was going fine. He hated Jesus and all his followers. He definitely didn't feel a need for Jesus. He very likely stood in the crowds listening to Jesus, confused and angry about why Jesus came after people like him with words like John 5:39–40: "You study the Scriptures diligently because you think that in them you have eternal life. These are the very Scriptures that testify about me, **yet you refuse to come to me** to have life" (emphasis mine). So yeah, Saul had a pretty strong resistance to work through if he was ever going to come to Jesus.

Saul persecuted the earliest followers of Jesus for spreading the crazy tale of his lordship and resurrection. He threw them in jail and approved of their murders. Well, at least he did until Jesus showed up. Saul (now Paul) later told people about what happened on that day:

> I saw a light from heaven, brighter than the sun, blazing around me and my companions. We all fell to the ground, and I heard a voice saying to me in Aramaic, "Saul, Saul, why do you persecute me? It is hard for you to kick against the goads." (Acts 26:13–14)

Saul had heard the voice of Jesus, and Jesus had used a fascinating expression: "kick against the goads." Goads were pointy spear-like instruments used by farmers in the fields to direct a stubborn ox. Occasionally the animal would kick at the goad. Those kicks weren't going to change the farmer's direction; they were only going to cause the animal more pain. It reminds me of when my parents used to say to my brothers and me when we were little, "We can do this the easy way, or we can do this the hard way." Despite how it seems in Scripture, Saul's encounter with Jesus was not out of the blue. Jesus had been working with Saul's stubborn resistance for years, pushing, prodding, and goading him in the direction God had set for him. What Saul realized on the road that day was that no amount of pride or anger was enough to keep him from the God who was drawing him in. He could kick against the goads, but it wouldn't change the fact that God wanted him.

He said, "No one can come to me unless the Father who sent me draws them" (John 6:44). If you have any desire to come to Jesus at all—even an aversion that makes you want to kick against him—you are being drawn by the Holy Spirit. Even if you aren't ready today to rearrange your week to make time for him, you are being drawn. If you hate everything I've said about needing the discipline of meeting in a time and place with Jesus, God is still after you. The Bible shows us a God who can influence the human heart in all its complexities, a God who somehow has the ability to draw you to him at your very core even as you kick against him in the process. I've learned to recognize that whenever I don't want to make the time to be with Jesus, *that's a thing.* Even my resistance to it means I am within the goads. I'm being drawn. I've learned to pray, *Help me come to you. I don't want to fight what you're doing.*

There's a God who will relentlessly pursue you, just like he did with Saul. You're being surrounded. I don't want you to kick against the goads. Make the time. Make the way. Ask him to help you. Because you're already being drawn in his direction. The final thing I want you to do—especially if you don't feel like it—is pray about the desire to show up. Ask yourself:

8. Am I willing to pray, *Help me want to come to you?*

Jesus said, "I am the bread of life. **Whoever comes to me** will never go hungry, and whoever believes in me will never be thirsty" (John 6:35, emphasis mine). Making time to come to Jesus has a promise attached: he will fill, strengthen, and satisfy you. He will literally sustain your life. Jesus wants you to come back again and again and again for the life you want.

He will not only answer this prayer, he will use other people to help you in the process. When I first came back to Jesus my life was a mess, and the craziest things started to happen: Christians started popping up everywhere! I was still in the corporate world at the time, and discovered my boss was a devoted Jesus-follower. After she learned about my faith she began to check in with me privately and encourage me toward God in my week. Another woman on my work team turned out to be a Christian too. She'd often share the books she was reading with me. I just blew it off as coincidence. Next, I ran into another acquaintance at church who I hadn't realized had any faith at all. I felt a little awkward, so I tried to avoid her, but she just wouldn't go away. It seemed everywhere I turned for a while, there she was! Neighbors, clients and partners of my husband, colleagues—everywhere I went, people seemed to mention Jesus or tell me about some part of their faith, their church, or their story. I was surrounded. Jesus was most definitely goading me in his direction through his people.

To sustain a pattern of showing up in your life, you need the encouragement of others who are trying to do the same. God may very well have already put some people around you! Open your eyes and ask yourself:

9. Who is in my life to encourage me to keep showing up?

Name the names. Tell them who they are. The more you can ask for and offer encouragement to bring yourself before Jesus, the better. The Christian life is not a solo sport. When you come to

Jesus, he offers you an entire body of believers to be connected to. I know the church isn't perfect, and many people have very real hurt from associating with churches of their past. I am so sorry for this hurt. Unfortunately, Jesus doesn't give us the option of giving up on his people because they are part of staying connected to him! Showing up in a community of Christ-followers is part of showing up to be with Jesus. They are your access point to experiencing the fullness of Jesus—his heart, mind, hands, feet, hugs, comfort, care, and service. The book of Ephesians talks about the body of Christ as a place where we grow into the maturity of our faith, experiencing Jesus among them.

> Then we will no longer be infants, tossed back and forth by the waves, and blown here and there by every wind of teaching and by the cunning and craftiness of people in their deceitful scheming. Instead, speaking the truth in love, we will grow to become in every respect the mature body of him who is the head, that is, Christ. (4:14–15)

Showing up to spend time connecting with Jesus will only survive if you do it both individually and within a community. So, the tenth question is:

10. What community of believers am I committed to showing up in?

Jesus has life for you, and it begins with showing up with your whole self and spending time together. Any connection in your life that matters was forged in a similar way with the support of a family, community, school, team, or group around it. Experiment. Be creative. Give yourself grace. But figure out how you're going to show up and be there.

TEN QUESTIONS FOR SHOWING UP

1. What day(s) of the week can I arrange time to myself?
2. What time(s) of the day could I get at least twenty uninterrupted minutes?
3. What is the place I will be in?
4. How long can I commit to keeping this time/place?
5. What will this cost me?
6. What are common external distractions for me?
7. What can I do to deal with these ahead of time?
8. Am I willing to pray, *Help me want to come to you*?
9. Who is in my life to encourage me to keep showing up?
10. What community of believers am I committed to showing up in?

3

TELL THE TRUTH

God is after your heart. When the Spirit pushes and prods you to come to Jesus, it is not primarily about you physically showing up. That sets up some necessary conditions, but coming to Jesus is really about your heart. Yes, your body needs to be involved, but the essence of *coming to him* goes to the core of your being. A strong foundation means you've got to go all the way in and all the way down. The wise builder digs as deep as he needs to in order to get to the rock. So when you show up, be ready to deal with the truth of your heart. And it's not always pretty in there.

In the Bible the heart is the very core and essence of the person and, therefore, the motivator of your actions, like in Proverbs 4:23: "Above all else, guard your heart, for everything you do flows from it." The endpoint of these three rhythms (come, hear, practice) is putting Jesus's words into action in your life. This means, according to the Bible, the process has to start inside the heart. When people from a modern, Western culture talk about the heart, it is often narrowed down to the source of our emotions. However, the Bible talks of the heart as a much more complex and dynamic center of our life, holding our wisdom, discernment, experience, emotions, convictions, and very source of life itself. In other words, our heart is where all our behaviors really start. What we do and say always has its origins there. Just before Jesus tells the parable of the wise and foolish builders, he makes this very point:

> No good tree bears bad fruit, nor does a bad tree bear good fruit. Each tree is recognized by its own fruit. People do not pick figs from thornbushes, or grapes from briers. A good man brings good things out of the good stored up in his heart, and an evil man brings evil things out of the evil stored up in his heart. For the mouth speaks what the heart is full of. (Luke 6:43–45)

When Jesus said these words, he pushed his listeners to acknowledge the truth of their own hearts by looking at what was coming out of their lives, pointing out their inconsistency: "Why do you call me, 'Lord, Lord,' and do not do what I say?" (Luke 6:46). Not only are all the things we do and say linked to what's going on in our hearts, but we have tremendous capacity for self-deception. We call Jesus Lord but maintain places in our lives where he clearly isn't. Jesus was driving his listeners to that truth. He didn't have their hearts and wanted them to see that too. If you want to know the truth about your own heart, there's a fail-proof method: look at the output in your life. Remember the foolish builder from our parable? There's no mention of him ever coming to Jesus. Jesus didn't have his heart. How do I know? **Because he didn't do anything.** "But the one who hears my words and does not put them into practice is like a man who built a house on the ground without a foundation" (Luke 6:49).

Something in our hearts has to happen *before* we encounter the Word of God or it won't ever produce fruit in our life. But if we involve our hearts? It's amazing what can happen then.

A couple years ago I stood in front of my bathroom sink doing my regular post-shower routine. First, facial moisturizer, then lotion, then deodorant, and finally I combed my hair. There are, of course, very specific and not-at-all-crazy reasons why I do it in precisely this order. As I made my way up and down my body with all my products, I caught myself doing the strangest thing: I avoided looking at certain body parts in the mirror. I kept my eyes fixed on the ones I approve of and glanced quickly away from the parts I have something against. There are some that used to be bigger or smaller or a different shape. Some I've held a grudge against for a lifetime for never once behaving the way I wanted. Their punishment? I simply wouldn't give them the time of day. Dead to me. I acted like they weren't even there.

We do that with our hearts too. There are parts that are bigger or smaller than we'd like. There are bitter parts that make us feel bad if we look at them too long. There are other parts that shriveled up and died a long time ago, so we avoid those altogether. And then there are the parts that misbehave. We can't control those, and sometimes we can't even predict what they'll do next! It's all very uncomfortable territory for a thinker like me; better to just glance quickly away and keep moving. After all, it's Tuesday, and I've got to get to work. I can just pick out a blouse that covers up that part.

As you might suspect, God is never satisfied with that approach. It leaves us unsteady, always susceptible to the winds and rising waters. So Jesus offered three rhythms to get us to firmer ground, starting with *come to me.* Come to me means seeing and being honest about what's going on in our hearts. The wise builder dug down deep to find the rock. Well, this is the digging part. We get straight into the crumbling places with our shovels, hoping there's a way to firmer ground. It starts with being willing to look at the places we'd rather not see.

When you make the time and space to show up, this is what I want you to do: acknowledge what you'd rather avoid. Tell Jesus the truth. With God, telling the truth is synonymous with opening up your heart to him. I've heard Christians say things like that and it frustrates me. What does opening your heart to God really mean? It's too obtuse for my taste, too much like embroidery on a pillow. In my experience, opening your heart to Jesus means this: show up and say honest things. Truth is the only starting point with God that encourages anything real to take place.

So what parts are you currently avoiding? Just this morning I was talking to God about something in my marriage that's troubled me off and on for a long time. I started considering a fast to really seek God about what he might say about it. An invitation to fast is just another kind of invitation to *come* to Jesus. Almost immediately I gave myself permission to ignore the suggestion. The truth is I don't want to fast because I am afraid. I am afraid of this messy, uncomfortable place. I'd rather pray prayers like *help us* rather than get further into it all. I'm afraid God won't answer me. I am afraid to hope that things will be different when it's been hard in that spot for a long time. I am afraid that if I come, he won't be there. My mind tried immediately to look away. I began thinking about something else, but I caught myself in the act of avoiding it as I made a silent, lame mental excuse about this not being a good week. I was trying to jump over the "come to me part" and have God dispense the answer in neat well-phrased bullet points, but that's not what he wants. He wants me to come to him. Sigh.

So I put the fast on my calendar for Thursday. I've learned to push myself into truthful places with God—or maybe, more precisely, I've learned to follow the Spirit into those places. The only reason I do is because of the irresistible promise of what's waiting there for me.

I will give you a new heart and put a new spirit in you; I will remove from you your heart of stone and give you a heart of flesh. And I will put my Spirit in you and move you to follow my decrees and

be careful to keep my laws. Then you will live in the land I gave
your ancestors; you will be my people, and I will be your God.
(Ezek. 36:26 28)

If I come to Jesus in truth, I get a new heart, for mine is weak
or crumbling or falling apart. This Scripture was written by the
prophet Ezekiel in reference to the coming, complete restoration
by the Messiah in the end. We get the amazing privilege of ac-
cessing the beginning of this fulfillment right now through his
Spirit at work in us! It's almost unreal that we have an offer on
the table to be restored and empowered by the Spirit of God. It's
an incredible thing God offers—to be equipped to obey him, to
be free enough and strong enough to put his words into practice
here and now. Instead of spending life looking away and avoiding
the crumbling places, we have the chance to start living with an
unbreakable foundation! And did you catch God's end goal? "You
will be my people, and I will be your God" (v. 28). His desire is
simply for us to come and be with him.

Jesus gave an invitation exactly like that to a man named
Zacchaeus (see Luke 19), who immediately recognized it for the
honor it was. Jesus invited himself over for dinner, and Zacchaeus
jumped at the chance to be near him. He, no doubt, never expected such an incredible opportunity. With his background as a
tax collector and a reputation for cheating people, he had plenty
of reasons to avoid an intimate experience with Jesus. But when
Jesus showed an interest in him, Zacchaeus saw what a big deal
it was. His heart was moved to tell the truth as he grasped at the
chance for a better life: "Look, Lord! Here and now I give half of
my possessions to the poor, and if I have cheated anybody out
of anything, I will pay back four times the amount" (Luke 19:8).
Zacchaeus openly acknowledged his character and his past. He
told the truth because the promise he saw in Jesus was too good
to pass up. Truth is the risky necessity to get Jesus's reward. But
it pays off every time.

The invitation to come into the presence of Jesus will always compel you toward the truth: his Spirit will move you to follow his decrees as Ezekiel said (see 36:27). When you make the time and space to come to him, I want you to ask yourself any of these four questions and just tell him the truth about the answer. See where it leads you.

What Is My *Craving*?

Tell Jesus the truth about what you really want from him. We all crave things we believe will help us to live deep, satisfied, fulfilled lives. Maybe there's a craving in your mind and heart, something you've wondered why God hasn't given to you already. Have the courage to say out loud exactly what you want Jesus to do. That kind of honesty and clarity usually moves us to a new place because things get real. Sometimes what we think we need crumbles under the weight and scrutiny of having to say it out loud. I've asked God for things that suddenly seem self-serving, unnecessary, or even deceitful, and I don't realize it until I tell him what I really want. And then sometimes admitting our craving actually breathes life into something that was put there by God himself. Telling the truth about it might just move us closer to having exactly what God already wants to give us.

I spent much of my adult life not putting words to the craving I had to speak and teach God's Word. When I finally began asking God for it, I realized it was precisely what his intentions were for me. One year I asked him to satisfy this craving through one teaching assignment a month for the entire year. I kept a folder on my computer with each teaching/speaking engagement, and at the end of the year I had thirteen! He gave me even more than I'd asked for. I no longer second-guessed my craving; admitting it was part of receiving it. God plants cravings in our hearts that he wants to fulfill and asks us the same question he asked a blind beggar who called to him on the road to Jericho one day:

> Jesus stopped and ordered the man to be brought to him. When he came near, Jesus asked him, **"What do you want me to do for you?"**
>
> "Lord, I want to see," he replied.
>
> Jesus said to him, "Receive your sight; your faith has healed you." Immediately he received his sight and followed Jesus, praising God. When all the people saw it, they also praised God. (Luke 18:40–43, emphasis mine)

This man's honest answer was the key to his craving being satisfied. Jesus wanted him to say it out loud. What. Do. You. Want?

What Is My *Confession*?

When I walked by the mirror in my house over twenty years ago and saw my own reflection, I started talking to myself, admitting the truth—first to myself, then to God. I had become someone I didn't know or like. As I said the awful words out loud, they turned into a prayer for forgiveness and a fresh start. I asked if he could change me. I will remember that moment for the rest of my life because God was there. I sensed my confession was somehow the key to something new between us. Now I know that telling the truth to myself and to God was the very thing that unlocked my ability to tell it to others and usher in the next chapter of my story. Honest confession put me in the right place with God. We mess up; he forgives. That's how it works. Sweeping things under the rug never accomplishes anything. Neither does making vows to never do something again or to be a better person from this point forward. New things with God stand on the rock of truth, so honest confession is the way to dig down and find a place to stand again. Jesus told a story about the connection between confession and coming before God to a bunch of people who'd probably never done it.

> Two men went up to the temple to pray, one a Pharisee and the other a tax collector. The Pharisee stood by himself and prayed: "God, I thank you that I am not like other people—robbers, evildoers, adulterers—or even like this tax collector. I fast twice a week and give a tenth of all I get."
> But the tax collector stood at a distance. He would not even look up to heaven, but beat his breast and said, "God, have mercy on me, a sinner."
> I tell you that this man, rather than the other, went home justified before God. For all those who exalt themselves will be humbled, and those who humble themselves will be exalted. (Luke 18:10–14)

This man's honest confession was his key to justification before God. You need to say it—out loud—so you can move on to the abundant life waiting for you with him.

What Is My *Confusion*?

Tell the truth to God about the places he doesn't make sense for you. God doesn't always work in ways we understand. His Word doesn't always sync with our minds and the patterns we've created for our lives. The days we live don't always unfold like we think they will, leaving confusion or frustration in the wake with unanswered questions. You might be sitting on a question for God that you really need to ask or a clarification of his heart, plans, or character. Ask! Ask like he can and will answer you. I have gone to Jesus in anguish and confusion and anger and disorientation.

When my kids were babies, I had a little meltdown while unloading the dishwasher because of an unasked and unanswered question. I yelled at God, "What am I doing? Why do you have me wasting my life and my gifts, locked away in this house, unloading the seven hundred eighty-fifth load of dishes this month? Is this what I get to do with my life?" Though it was not my finest moment, it was definitely—finally—the question I needed to ask God. Jesus answers honest questions.

He did the same for a guy named Nicodemus who came one night seeking answers about something confusing Jesus had said:

> "Very truly I tell you, no one can see the kingdom of God unless they are born again."
>
> "How can someone be born when they are old?" Nicodemus asked. "Surely they cannot enter a second time into their mother's womb to be born!"
>
> Jesus answered, "Very truly I tell you, no one can enter the kingdom of God unless they are born of water and the Spirit. Flesh gives birth to flesh, but the Spirit gives birth to spirit." (John 3:3–6)

The conversation went on from there. Jesus met Nicodemus exactly where he was in what he was asking, and he also wanted him to come closer and ask more questions. Jesus had more to teach him. More to say to him. He has more for you too. Ask! Your honest question might be the key to an authentic interaction with God that leads you to more. You don't have to know exactly what you're asking; Jesus will lead you from wherever you are to the answers you need. Come and be honest about your confusion.

What Is My *Curiosity*?

Tell the truth to God about what you'd like to see and experience *of him.* Do you want to know what it's like to hear his voice or feel his Spirit? Do you wonder if he could heal something in your body? Are you curious if your dream meant something? Curiosities lurk in our minds about the supernatural, spiritual realm of existence that is so clearly present in the Bible.

Sometimes, curiosities are purposeful to pique your mind and heart into an encounter with a supernatural God in the midst of your very normal life. If you get honest and speak the little thoughts in the back of your mind, you may just open new possibilities with a God who is in the business of the incredible, the miraculous, the unbelievable. Talk to God about the things you feel a little crazy for even saying out loud. Pause and wonder about him.

Coming to Jesus in curiosity means having a willingness to suspend what you previously thought you knew and to consider what might be possible with God. You have the opportunity to explore a life with God beyond your experience, your mind, your preconceived notions. Maybe you need to set aside a way you've always done something or thought about him. Maybe other people's thoughts or opinions or even your own emotions have been in the way of getting honest like this. Coming to God through open curiosity is considering whether Jesus could be the key to explaining or experiencing something you didn't even think possible. If you find yourself saying, "Could God really do this?" then lean into that thought. Because *what if he could*? What if your curiosities are the crumbs of the Holy Spirit, thrown out to see if you will notice them and be brave enough to walk toward a more complete truth about God?

This happened to me when I stood in my kitchen years ago, and a little laugh escaped from my lips. I said out loud, "Could it really be true, God? Is that a real thing?" I was alone and turning over and over in my mind what someone had said to me that day at work. I had just started my first job in ministry and a colleague pulled me aside and said, "You have a gift. You're hearing the Holy Spirit speak to you and you don't even know it." This new possibility bubbled up inside me and burst out in a little laugh. It delighted me. I felt an effervescence as I considered the possibility of a Spirit who actively communicated with me. What if it were true? Could it be? At the time, it was an exciting and new thought about God, and it has now become a part of how I live and breathe. God wants to take you to a fuller life and more truth. Your unique curiosity is part of how he'll lead you there.

Peter considered the same type of thing one night with Jesus, and it led him to something he never thought would be possible.

> The boat was already a considerable distance from land, buffeted by the waves because the wind was against it.
>
> Shortly before dawn Jesus went out to them, walking on the lake. When the disciples saw him walking on the lake, they were terrified. "It's a ghost," they said, and cried out in fear.
>
> But Jesus immediately said to them: "Take courage! It is I. Don't be afraid."
>
> "Lord, if it's you," Peter replied, "tell me to come to you on the water."
>
> **"Come," he said.**
>
> Then Peter got down out of the boat, walked on the water and came toward Jesus. (Matt. 14:24–29, emphasis mine)

Peter's willingness to explore his curiosity was the key to an incredible encounter with the power of Jesus.

Paul wrote a prayer in his Letter to the Ephesians that they would continue to grow in their experience and knowledge of a supernatural, powerful God. His prayer is for you too.

> I keep asking that the God of our Lord Jesus Christ, the glorious Father, may give you the Spirit of wisdom and revelation, so that you may know him better. I pray that the eyes of your heart may be enlightened in order that you may know the hope to which he has called you, the riches of his glorious inheritance in his holy people, and his incomparably great power for us who believe. That power is the same as the mighty strength he exerted when he raised Christ from the dead and seated him at his right hand in the heavenly realms, far above all rule and authority, power

and dominion, and every name that is invoked, not only in the present age but also in the one to come. And God placed all things under his feet and appointed him to be head over everything for the church, which is his body, the fullness of him who fills everything in every way. (1:17–23)

Your cravings, confessions, confusions, or curiosities might be just the places you need to go through in order to really come to Jesus in truth. You may be tempted to overlook these very places out of fear, pain, or uncertainty about yourself and about God. But these four things have the power to move you to new depths. You don't have to know exactly where it might take you; just show up and start telling the truth.

4

KNEEL DOWN

I hate unloading the dishwasher, so maybe I was already irritated. I yelled at God about wasting my life as I did the dishes. I felt like I was shriveling up. My brain hadn't been used to calculate anything except how many minutes until the next breastfeeding for about a year. I yearned to learn, read, work, and wear clothes that were more than a half step above pj's. As much as I loved all my babies, I was tired of living my days in the forty-five-minute cycles of naps, feedings, and preschool schedules for four tiny humans, the same ones who dirtied all those dishes.

I was mad at God. He was the one who'd sent me to stay home and stand in the kitchen at the sink. I'd quit my paying job a few years before to work full-time at home caring for our ever-growing number of kids. It seemed like it was what God wanted for us when I did it. We'd prayed and carefully considered the change. On my best days I saw the purpose and beauty in this season, but not on this day. I didn't want to hear it. I felt numb and then angry. If this was God's plan, then he must not have known me very well. All I could see that day were the things that had died—the jobs and opportunities and the relationships connected to them; the travel and fun and my old dreams about what I'd be doing at this point in my life. It felt like the world was moving on without me, and the future I'd imagined was gone. I knew I wasn't looking at it all clearly, but I was overwhelmed with the idea that I could no longer picture my life even a couple years in the future. I'd given up a corporate career to go into ministry, and then I'd given up ministry for dishes. I was out of plans.

Not long after my dishwasher meltdown, I had an interaction with God I will never forget. I can't decide if it was sad or beautiful. Probably both. I came to him one day with all my anger and sadness and blindness over the future. I closed my eyes as I nursed my baby and suddenly imagined I was holding a heart— a beating human heart—in my hands. It represented all that I'd wanted, worked for, and called my own, all the dreams I thought we shared for my life. In my imagination I gently set the heart on the floor, and—terrified—I watched the beating slow down. I said to God, "I give up. I can't keep this alive anymore. It's not working. I don't know what you're doing with my life, but if there's something more you want then you'll have to keep it alive." In my half-asleep/half-awake state, I pushed the heart toward God and watched the beating come to a stop. As I turned my back, I glimpsed a last flutter of a heartbeat as it lay there on the ground. I walked away.

That was the day I moved on. I didn't pine for the past or strain toward the future anymore. I cared for my babies, slowly learned to love being at home, and even more slowly arrived at peace with this phase of life I never planned for myself. For the next couple of years, every now and then, I'd close my eyes and see that heart again in a dream or while I was praying. I was never sure if it had completely stopped or if I had caught a glimpse of a tiny, almost imperceptible heartbeat.

"Stop *striving* and know that I am God" (Ps. 46:10 NASB).

To Come Is to Give Up Your Plan

To give up your own plan is to kneel before Jesus. It might be your plan for today. It might be for the timing of the relationship you're in, or for the big-picture direction you thought your life was going in. Big or small, your plan is *your* plan. Coming to Jesus means giving up the way you'd do it if you were in charge.

The day I gave up I felt a little relieved. I had tried so hard to keep possibilities alive in my life. Setting that heart down and walking away felt both sad and freeing. I came to realize my biggest fear was, What if I trusted God with my future and he really didn't have anything good planned? I was terrified that my doing the dishes was his big plan for me. I also knew I couldn't keep holding on to what I thought my life was going to be. It clearly wasn't going to happen that way. If I wanted God, I was going to have to risk finding out if he'd come through with a way forward. I didn't know how to do it for myself anymore, except to start by saying, "Okay, I give up." So I knelt.

Another woman also came to Jesus about her future. She, too, had suffered enough. She "had been subject to bleeding for twelve years. She had suffered a great deal under the care of many doctors and had spent all she had, yet instead of getting better she grew worse" (Mark 5:25–26). My little meltdown at the sink made me wonder if the morning she came to Jesus she'd had her own meltdown. Who could blame her? Bleeding for *twelve years*. We ladies have a special understanding of just how awful that would be. Of course, it would have been hard to manage physically, but worse, it would have made her ritually unclean. In the Jewish culture that meant she couldn't live a normal life, go to temple, be in the community. It was a huge deal. The day she came to Jesus, she was at the end of the road. She was desperate. So desperate, in fact, that she pushed her way through a crowd toward Jesus, army-crawl style. Picture playing hide-and-seek behind the couch and trying to stay low and out of sight; that's what she was likely doing in the crowd. She was trying to stay invisible because she wasn't supposed to be there. Except she *had* to come. Jesus was the one person who could change her future.

But here's the thing: even though it was brave of her to come that day, she still came on her own terms. She was planning to do it her way, hoping she could get what she came for and walk away. I'm sure the risk of rejection probably seemed too great to try it face-to-face, so she "came up behind him in the crowd and touched his cloak, because she thought, 'If I just touch his clothes, I will be healed'" (vv. 27–28).

It worked! She got what she came for, but Jesus had something else in mind. To get her to it, Jesus had to help her do more than just show up. She was going to have to willingly kneel down. Jesus wanted her to actually, fully *come to him*. This woman didn't just need a zap of miraculous power, she needed *Jesus*.

When I first considered what Jesus did next, it almost seemed mean. He stopped and demanded to know who touched him (v. 30). I initially thought, *Why make the poor woman stand up in front of everyone? You know she was healed. Hadn't she been through enough?* But then I realized what Jesus was doing; he was giving her the opportunity to really come to him, to show up, kneel down willingly, and see what he might do. He was giving her the chance to decide if she wanted her plan or his.

The Scriptures say she came terrified and "fell at his feet" (v. 33). At his insistence, she stood up and told everyone what had just happened to her. Because of her public testimony that day, authenticated by Jesus and witnessed by the crowd, this woman who'd been ostracized and in pain for twelve years was not just physically healed, she was going to get her whole life back! Crawling through the crowd and slinking away wasn't enough for Jesus. He wanted it *all* for her—the relationships, the temple, the family—he wanted to give her *life*. But first, she had to show up. She had to fight through her fear and tell the truth. She had to fall at the feet of Jesus and see what happened next. After she told the truth, Jesus responded, "Your faith has healed you. Go in peace" (v. 34). To get the fullness of the life Jesus wanted for her, she had to set aside her own plan and kneel before him.

■ **Use this prayer, crafted from Philippians 3:4–12, when it's time to let go of your plan:**

Lord, I am ready to stop putting confidence in my own plan and what I've been holding on to for myself. I thought I was good and strong and capable, but now I wonder if there is more I could have in you. Letting go of the plans I was holding on to is now in my way of coming to you. I am willing to lose this, even though it's important to me. I know the most important thing I can do is come to you. Even if it means some sort of death, I want all the life you have for me. Amen.

To Come Is to Give Up Your Power

Before I had all those babies who dirtied all the dishes, I remember dating my husband and going to a Catholic Mass for the first time with his family. At some point during the hour, they suddenly pulled down a little padded bench on hinges below the pew. I hadn't noticed the benches when we walked in, so I was amazed to suddenly see every person hit their knees at once. To them it was no big deal, but I was struck by the beautiful picture of how we are supposed to come before Jesus. *We kneel.*

Kneeling is always about giving up power. I've seen plenty of period films on PBS to know how it works: you go before the king on the throne, and as you approach him, you kneel down. You take a powerless position as an act of trust. As the back of your neck is exposed, you quite literally put your life in his hands, knowing that the king could either bless you or cut off your head. Even the friends of a king knelt in his presence.

> For dominion belongs to the LORD
> and he rules over the nations.

All the rich of the earth will feast and worship;
    all who go down to the dust will kneel before him—
    those who cannot keep themselves alive.

(Ps. 22:28–29)

When we come to Jesus, we acknowledge that we really cannot live life on our own power. The King has more, and you need it. The day I put down the beating heart, I admitted my own strength wasn't going to cut it. Others also fell at the feet of Jesus; it wasn't just the bleeding woman. They needed help or saving or healing and saw he had the power. Jesus's friend Mary fell at his feet when her brother Lazarus died. She said, "Lord, if you had been here, my brother would not have died" (John 11:32). In other words, "Jesus, you are the one with the power to give life. Not me."

Giving up power to Jesus hasn't come for me in one big, grand gesture. It's happened one little part of my life at a time as I've gotten weak or tired or I've just plain done a bad job of it. I've learned to come to Jesus more quickly when I feel that now. I say, "Whoops! I'm trying to do it all on my own strength again." I've come to him asking for power to be a better wife, to manage friendships, to do my job. You can be sure that before every word of this book I said to him, "I need you or I just can't." I keep finding new places where I'm trying it on my own and finding out I'm not enough.

The day I threw the dishes into the sink, I was wrestling with whether I'd given power to someone who was really using it for my good. It didn't feel like it at the time, so my reaction was *I'll keep what little I've got, thank you very much.* But Jesus can be trusted. He put a very different picture of power on display in his life over and over again. He used it to speak life, heal sickness, and set people free. He taught his disciples to be the kind of people who don't lord power over others, but who use it to serve them instead. His life was a picture of a God you could trust with power over your life.

■ **Use this prayer, crafted from Ephesians 1:18–22, in moments or days you need to hand power back to Jesus:**

Lord, open my eyes to the hope and the future and the power I have access to in you. Help me stop believing anything else will ever be able to do what you can in my life. I want the power at work in my life to be your unique power—a power that can bring life to anyone and anything. I give up doing it with my own strength. I give up the things I was clinging to for my power or control. Come be the authority you truly are, the one who's above every position and name and kingdom here on earth. Jesus, I see that you—and only you—can be trusted with that in my life. Amen.

To Come Is to Meet at the Cross

When you decide it's time to give up your plans or your power, there's a place you need to go: the cross.

It's crazy that we wear crosses around our necks and hang them on our walls. I'm looking at a cross made of beautiful swirly wood in my room right now. A cross was an executioner's tool. The modern equivalent of a cross necklace would be a gold electric chair charm or a silver syringe hanging around your neck. Weird. The cross was the pinnacle of guilt, shame, pain, and death, but somehow Jesus turned it into the very opposite. Now we see it as a place of beauty, mercy, and grace. That's the place you're invited to come and kneel.

But where is that, exactly? It sometimes makes me crazy when Christians say things like, "Just come to the cross." I mean—for real—the last one I saw with my own eyes was in a cornfield beside a highway driving through Ohio with a sign next to it that said, "Hell is Real."

Is that where you need to go?

Not quite.

When I say you have to meet Jesus at the cross, I mean it the way the Bible uses that location. The cross is the place where you access the power of God (1 Cor. 1:18). It's the place of reconciliation between you and God and you and others (Eph. 2:16). The cross is the place you make peace with God (Col. 1:20), because it's where the debt you owe God for your sin is canceled and the charges of guilt that would condemn you are dropped (Col. 2:14). The cross is the place of victory over any other power or authority in your life (Col. 2:15), and it's the spot where religious rule keepers will always be offended at the radical freedom and grace you can get while you're there (Gal. 5:11).

That's what I mean. You come to the cross because *those* are the things you're after.

I want you to draw one here. Sometimes I do this in my journal, so it feels more like a real place.

Now imagine walking up to it just as you are today—a mix of contentment and anxiety, a blend of happiness and pain, some bad memories you're trying not to think about, some unhealed relationships that are just limping along, with some control issues and coping mechanisms you secretly worry about too. Walk up with all of that to meet Jesus at the cross. And kneel down because you trust that he's going to be good to you. Kneel down knowing he could take your life. Kneel down knowing his plans are always resurrection at the cross! It was *there* that Jesus won back all authority over you, so he will use his power to serve you and bring you life.

Don't hesitate to come—especially if you need to confess, let go, sacrifice, or give up—if it feels like some sort of death. At the cross you go *through* death into life. The day I broke the plate in the sink (did I mention that before?) I was focused on the pain of what I'd lost. I was busy mulling over the ugliness of my house and my body and the diapers. All I could see was the death—the diapers and dishes and isolation. I forgot that with Jesus, life always goes straight through death. That day I stumbled to the foot of the cross.

You're going to have to choose over and over again whether to kneel down. Will it be his plan or yours? His power or yours? His life or yours? When I pushed that imaginary beating heart across the ground to him, it felt like the end of something. And it was. I just had no idea that in the kingdom of God the end is always just the beginning. Jesus can turn anything that was supposed to be against you and use it as the very mechanism of your blessing! The cross was meant to be the brutal end of life, but now we dip it in gold and wear it on a chain because it is the very opposite.

There were two prisoners on crosses next to Jesus. All the first prisoner saw was Jesus's shameful death—and he mocked it. He was blind to the power and plans of God that were taking place on that cross. "Aren't you the Messiah? Save yourself and us!" (Luke 23:39). But the other one bowed before Jesus there. He truly came to him with the words "Jesus, remember me when you come into your kingdom" (23:42). He bowed down at the cross, recognizing it for what it was: the amazing power and plans of God to bring new life.

When you kneel before Jesus at the cross, what you're going to get back is grace. *Grace* is the undeserved favor of someone who's above you. Grace is the blessing of a King. And grace only flows *down*. If you want it, you'll have to kneel!

Grace is the solid ground you'll find for building the rest of your life upon. Grace is the type of rock that makes the best foundation. Grace from the cross cannot be shaken. Paul writes, "By the grace God has given me, I laid a foundation as a wise builder" (1 Cor. 3:10). The foundation you need to build your life on is made of grace. The wise builder kneels at the cross for grace because it is the unbreakable rock you can stand back up on. Coming to Jesus means you can build a life stronger and better than any you could create on your own.

If you're ready for that kind of grace, it's time to kneel.

Like, literally, do it.

Kneel.

Then, pray this prayer crafted from the words of Revelation 1:17–18:

Jesus, I am here at your feet. Some things feel like they are dying in my life. I know I do not need to be afraid because of you. You are the first and the last. You are the living One. You were dead, and now you are alive for ever and ever. You are the key for anything in my life to come alive. I want the life you offer me at the cross. Show me how to receive your grace. Amen.

Okay, great! Kneeling also happens to put you in the perfect position to *hear* the voice of Jesus, so let's keep going. "Give ear and come to me; listen, that you may live" (Isa. 55:3).

PART 2

HEAR

Fifteen years ago I reached for a wine glass in the corner cabinet and found myself randomly thinking about John the Baptist. As I picked up the glass, Luke 1:15 popped into my brain: "He is never to take wine or other fermented drink, and he will be filled with the Holy Spirit even before he is born." I thought it was an odd verse to randomly come to mind, so I blew it off. The next day I reached for my drink when I was out to dinner and again heard "John the Baptist took no wine or other fermented drink." It took a moment to register the second appearance of this verse in as many days. I tilted my head—were these words from God somehow?

I thought this John the Baptist verse might be God's way of trying to say something to me. Given the context, I decided it had something to do with drinking alcohol. I don't believe God hates wine, so I wasn't prone to take it as some sort of scolding for having a glass with dinner. I had to decide, *Was* this God? And, if so, what did he want? I wasn't drinking a lot. I wasn't getting drunk. But I had to admit the verse did appear to mean something about not drinking. I didn't love that, but I was eager to connect with God. I decided to launch a little experiment: I'd stop drinking for a few weeks and see if I got any more insight. Lent was near, and my husband grew up Catholic so he usually gave up something for forty days. I joined him and gave up alcohol. Forty days seemed plenty long enough to hear something more. Jesus himself probably would have had to turn my wine into water if he wanted me to go longer. The forty days came and went; nothing really happened.

Not long after this John the Baptist thing I found myself pregnant with my second baby. It wasn't until about nine months later, as he was born, that I had a sudden thought about the timing of conception. I had gotten pregnant three-ish weeks after I'd stopped drinking. I couldn't shake the thought that they were somehow connected. Did God know something I didn't? Was it related to alcohol, my body, and babies? I didn't know for sure, but the thought nagged me.

Years before that, I was diagnosed with a fertility condition. I was a mild case and got pregnant not long after the diagnosis, so I never researched much beyond what the doctors first told me. I also didn't have the internet in our pocket to google every medical condition like I would now. But, because of my nagging thought, I looked further into it.

Turns out, God *did* know something I didn't.

My fertility challenge was connected to my body's (in)ability to process certain types of sugars—sugars exactly like the ones found in alcohol. I thought about this for a long time. Could it really be that hearing and responding to an odd verse about John the Baptist impacted my whole life? I thought, *Surely that's not how God works, is it?!*

"Give ear and come to me; listen, that you may live" (Isa. 55:3).

The life God has for you is connected to hearing his words. He wants you to hear his Word so he can bring you life. The volume and intensity with which you hear his Word are directly correlated with the pages of the Bible. You will hear the *living* Word of God louder and more frequently as you encounter the *written* Word of God. In this case, it seemed God had given me a literal life as a result of hearing his words and trying to do something with them. As surreal as it seemed, I was certain this is what had happened.

It's also exactly what Jesus taught. The day Jesus told the parable of the wise and foolish builders there was a big crowd gathered to listen to the Sermon on the Mount. Because of the natural acoustics of the spot, his words reached thousands of ears. People physically listened, but fewer actually *heard* the sermon. He finished it by saying, "**As for everyone who comes to me and hears my words and puts them into practice,** I will show you what they are like. They are like a man building a house, who dug down deep and laid the foundation on rock. When a flood came, the torrent struck that house but could not shake it, because it was well built" (Luke 6:47–48, emphasis mine).

Come first. Hear second. The second rhythm on the way to a well-built life is "Hear my words." It is the instruction sandwiched between the other two rhythms; it is the hinge. We *come* to Jesus in order to *hear his words* of life, and we must *hear* something from him to *practice* following him.

Jesus saw that the Pharisees spent years memorizing God's words in the Hebrew Scriptures, and yet it hadn't given them true life: "You study the Scriptures diligently because you think that in them you have eternal life. These are the very Scriptures that testify about me, yet you refuse to **come to me** to have life" (John 5:39–40, emphasis mine).

Hearing only leads to life when the Word reaches a soft, open heart. The prophet Ezekiel first made clear what Jesus also said: the state of our heart can essentially make us blind and deaf to God (see Ezek. 12:2). In other words, *hearing is only worth something if you've first come to him.* And no one comes to Jesus without the Spirit of God drawing them. The work of the Spirit in your life will cause you to come to Jesus with your whole heart. When you do, you receive what Jesus called "ears to hear" (see v. 2).

Ears to hear is an expression that goes back to prophets like Ezekiel and Moses as a description of the ability to discern God and his truths. Jesus echoed this phrase many times as he taught in parables. Those whose hearts were ready and willing were able to hear the truths of the parable because they were discerned by the Spirit. Ears to hear can function only in the kingdom of God and only with an open and willing heart. This phrase is always connected with a desire to obey God. Ears to hear are compelled to put into practice what they are hearing. Hearing is the hinge between coming to Jesus and putting his words into practice. Ears to hear are at the heart and center of the everyday rhythms of come, hear, practice.

> **But the one who hears my words and does not put them into practice** is like a man who built a house on the ground without a foundation. The moment the torrent struck that house, it collapsed and its destruction was complete. (Luke 6:49, emphasis mine)

Ears that cannot hear are always associated with hard hearts. Hard hearts are skeptical and unlikely to obey. They don't do experiments to see if they can find God. Deaf ears are found on those who either cannot or will not accept and understand God's ways. The prophets accused Israel of not having ears to hear at times when they were in open rebellion against the Lord. Many of the people who heard the Sermon on the Mount were the same ones who said they believed in God. They didn't (yet) have ears to hear.

That was me.

For years I didn't actively reject the words of Jesus or the Bible; I just didn't understand why it all mattered so much. I thought it was enough that I believed in God. So I built my early adult life in a way that made sense to me—on Gen X–style independence and success. I got it, but it nearly killed my marriage and ruined my character. Luckily, I crashed.

I do mean luckily. It was only when the ground fell out beneath me that I got the proof I needed that none of it was ever going to work. My crash sent me back to ground zero to figure out how to do it differently—life, marriage, work, and character. The greatest gift God has ever given me is experiencing *exactly* the fall warned about in this parable. I went seeking mercy and forgiveness. I became needy and started looking, desperate for direction, and I welcomed the Spirit into my life. I put all my eggs in the Jesus basket because there was nowhere else I could turn. For the first time, I received my ears to hear. And as I tested, tried, obeyed, and experimented, I encountered the truth of what Jesus taught: it's only **his** words, *heard and practiced*, that can build a life on solid ground.

The words you need are not inside your own head. They aren't in your inner goddess. They aren't in good moral thinking or in talk show self-help or in the words of new philosophies or inspiring memes. They're in the Bible. And they're breathed out for you daily by the Holy Spirit. "The grass withers and the flowers fall, but the word of our God endures forever" (Isa. 40:8). The Word of God won't erode in floods or trouble. The rock you need under your life is the written and living Word.

And good news! There are ways to encourage the strength and volume of the Spirit in your life. The next few chapters are about training your ears to hear and hearing regularly. Once received, you need to use 'em. The book of Hebrews acknowledges this. It is written to *believers*, and they are being warned against unbelief! They already believed, but they needed to regularly hear God's words with a soft, open heart. Believers, it's time to believe you have ears to hear. You need to use them on a regular basis. "So, as the Holy Spirit says: 'Today, if you hear his voice, do not harden your hearts as you did in the rebellion'" (Heb. 3:7–8).

There's a living God, and if you're in Christ, you have the ears to hear him! To open and train them for use, I want you to quiet down, have a plan, and learn your story.

I don't want you to miss a single word that God has to say.

5

QUIET DOWN

I am sitting in my study right now. My house is quiet. At least it seems so at first. When I listen more closely there are quite a few sounds: the washing machine filling up three rooms away, the air blowing through the vent, the tweeting of birds outside, and the occasional thump of my cat jumping against the window as the birds seemingly taunt her. Small repetitive noises drive me nuts. If I fixated on them, I wouldn't be able to work; but somehow, nearly all of it falls to the background.

In a few hours, when my four kids get home, there will be new layers of noise: laughing, talking, piano playing, kissing sounds at the cat, squabbling over the iPad, boots stomping, blenders making smoothies, toilets flushing, and a *Say Yes to the Dress* episode airing on TV. Someone will be yelling "Mom" every forty-two seconds, keeping me from having a full thought. It gets loud.

But the loudest thing I've ever experienced was an Ohio State football game at the home stadium, otherwise known as "the Horseshoe." The deafening noise was a compilation of the half-drunk student section, the huge marching band, and the waves of O-H-I-O cheers from 105,000 screaming people. I didn't fully understand home field advantage until I watched another team penalized for delay of game because they couldn't hear their own quarterback standing right beside them. Even still, at a game one Saturday, right in the midst of all that noise, I fell asleep on my husband's shoulder.

I fell *asleep*.

How does that even *happen*?

It's because of the tipping point. The point where there is so much noise, so loud, for so long, that you don't hear anything at all. The cacophony of sounds blends together and none of it means anything. That day, I went past the tipping point and just dropped off into the white noise.

Spiritually, you live inside the Horseshoe, and you've nodded off. You can't hear God because you're constantly surrounded by words being yelled at you on social media, entertainment, twenty-four-hour news, and online information of unimaginable depth—not to mention the advertisements alongside any words you're reading. The phone in your pocket demands twenty-four-hour availability for word-based communication with more people than you were built to handle! I once learned the average human capacity for relationships is about 150 (with less than 15 of them as actual friends), but you're connected to thousands and thousands of people online. And they *all* like to talk! You can't even hear your own thoughts—let alone God. There are just too many words. If you want to hear the Holy Spirit—the voice and words of God in your life—then you're going to have to quiet things down a bit.

You have a tipping point, and staying away from it is critical to following Jesus. The words of God will have whatever space you leave them in the deafening noise of your days. A strong foundation for your life requires regular, authentic exchanges between you and your Father through the Holy Spirit. That has to happen somehow in your everyday life. If you want to follow Jesus, you have to lower the volume enough to hear him.

Jesus needed to get away from the noise too. He wanted to give his Father his full attention so he could really hear him and follow his lead. The night before Jesus appointed his twelve disciples, the Bible says he "went out to a mountainside to pray, and spent the night praying to God. When morning came, he called his disciples to him and chose twelve of them" (Luke 6:12–13). Getting away to quiet things down was undoubtedly connected to making this big decision. Jesus surely wanted to hear what his Father had to say! He came to get counsel, wisdom, clarity, and direction—all the things we want God to give us too. To get them, Jesus deliberately lowered the volume in the world around him and gave the Spirit the margin to speak. It wasn't just this once; Jesus withdrew regularly to meet quietly with his Father.

Most of the times I've accused God of being silent, it's more likely that I just wasn't able to hear him over all the noise. There are six of us at family dinner in my house, so there's a lot of talking. My husband burst out laughing when we were at the table one night and I asked, "Why in the world would someone think it's a good idea to make *Die Hard* a musical?!" He'd said that the movie *Die Hard* was going to be on Broadway this Christmas. Or at least that's what I thought I heard. You can imagine the difficulty I was having with what sort of show tunes those might be. What he *actually* said was that *Die Hard* was going to be on Bravo—*not* Broadway—this Christmas. Yes, the movie is questionable, but at least Bravo made a lot more sense. I just couldn't hear him over all the noise, even from a few feet away. With a little bit of quiet, it's amazing how many fewer times you'll think God is silent or Bruce Willis is going to be on Broadway with a machine gun at Christmastime.

Given that you probably won't start by going to a mountainside to pray (though that's a great idea), let's talk about how you could introduce some quiet into your life.

Leave the Stadium

The first thing you need to do is stand up and walk out of the stadium on a regular basis. Hearing the voice of the Spirit requires backing away from your tipping point of words with pockets of lower volume and silence. Life is so loud; silence won't happen unless you create it on purpose. Only in a quieter place do individual sounds and words become audible again. Only outside the stadium can you even begin to separate all the different sounds and words that are in your mind and heart.

I understand there is a concept in the process of physical hearing called *auditory attention*; it's the ability we develop as we learn to speak that allows us to sort through sounds and assign them categories of importance. To talk, we figure out that some sounds are more important than others. Some noises we need to pay close attention to, and others we need to let fade to the background. This concept is the reason why I can still work and write with all those irritating little noises going on around me at home. I instinctively sort them and let some fade. Without a quiet enough environment to learn and practice prioritizing and sorting sounds in, we might just fixate on the air blowing through the vent. Our spiritual ears need to be cultivated in the same way. They need to be trained to cut through the background noise and focus on the most important words. And that takes some quiet.

Start by choosing some moments when you can simply give your physical ears a break. Think of your ears as the gateway to your mind and heart. Pick some moments when you don't let anything new in. You don't have to make this super spiritual; do whatever you were going to do—just do it in silence. It's become pretty common for most of us to have two devices and two different audio inputs happening at any given time. Social media and Hulu, music and texting, work laptop and a podcast. You have learned to operate on overload, so it may be uncomfortable to back off. It might even feel like something is wrong, like you're not doing enough. But when your physical ears (and eyes) get a break from the words, your spiritual ears start to work better. It gives margin for the voice of God in your day.

The biggest and most important low-volume habit in my life is starting the day in the quiet. I don't want to hear anything. I even got my youngest kid headphones for the iPad for when she wakes up super early. I don't want to hear her show at six o'clock in the morning. Sometimes I literally take a few minutes to just sit in the silence. I invite God into this time. I don't have my phone because soon I'm distracted by all the words there—email, social media, calendars, playlists, all words vying for my attention. Sometimes I also drive in silence when I'm alone in the car, and I almost always run without headphones. These are small ways I lower the volume. Maybe you can keep the TV off in your house or experiment with small breaks from phones, watches, social media, or texting. There's so much noise with your devices that even thirty minutes without one of them can help you back away from the tipping point. You'd be surprised how many words are already inside you! You are full, and sorting through the sounds only happens in the quiet.

Stop the Hum

As it gets a bit quieter you will probably notice a constant humming. The hum can get loud enough to prevent you from clearly hearing the words of Jesus for you. It's your list of *shoulds*. The hum of shoulds causes you to overlook the need to hear his words and pushes us too soon to action. This hum doesn't want to prevent you from stopping to hear Jesus and jump quickly into doing whatever *you* think he's going to say.

Jesus came to stay at the house of a woman named Martha who was consumed by this sort of hum. A group had gathered and was listening to Jesus speak. Hospitality was a big deal in Jewish culture, so Martha was working very hard. She got frustrated with her sister Mary, who wasn't helping at all. Instead of doing the work she *should* have been doing, Mary was sitting at the feet of Jesus, simply listening.

I feel Martha's pain here. I want people to be fed and cared for in my home, and hosting is hard work. Martha asked Jesus to back her up. All she wanted was a little help from Mary. I'm sure she was expecting Jesus to agree. It does seem right, doesn't it? She wanted Jesus to tell Mary to do the right thing (aka the stuff she *should* be doing), so Martha was probably shocked when Jesus responded differently. "'Martha, Martha,' the Lord answered, 'you are worried and upset about many things, but few things are needed—or indeed only one. Mary has chosen what is better, and it will not be taken away from her'" (Luke 10:41–42).

You don't need to do all the things before you stop and hear the words of Jesus. Mary wasn't doing what she *should* have been doing. She was trying to hear Jesus instead. As soon as you try to get quiet and hear what Jesus is saying, someone is going to come at you with what you should be doing instead.

The Pharisees often criticized Jesus for implying that he took his direction straight from God. When they gave him a hard time about that, Jesus answered them: "It is written in the Prophets: 'They will all be taught by God.' Everyone who has heard the Father and learned from him comes to me" (John 6:45). You can come to Jesus and hear your Father. Have the audacity to think you can actually hear God's voice! You absolutely can. Insist on the time and space in your life to do it. You have to stop the hum of busily meeting expectations and doing the right things before you ever stop and listen.

Shoulds will harass you with tasks that keep you from Jesus. They try to take the place of your sitting at the feet of your Father and hearing specific, personal words from him. Shoulds become a religious checklist that bypasses the need to hear from the Spirit at all. Religion tells you that hearing the Spirit isn't necessary—just do what you should. But Jesus would rather you come and hear what he has to say *first* before you start working, cleaning, cooking, and serving. Jesus came to walk with you and talk you through whatever you're doing, one day at a time. He did not bring you a to-do list. Shoulds are a hum that tries to drown out the voice of Jesus saying to you,

> Are you tired? Worn out? Burned out on religion? Come to me. Get away with me and you'll recover your life. I'll show you how to take a real rest. Walk with me and work with me—watch how I do it. Learn the unforced rhythms of grace. I won't lay anything heavy or ill-fitting on you. Keep company with me and you'll learn to live freely and lightly. (Matt. 11:28–30 MSG)

The hum makes you feel like you have to do all the work of digging a foundation and building your life alone. You don't! Getting your work done is good. Caring for others is good. Helping out and serving is good. Jesus may speak to you about doing one of these things, or all of them in due time, but no checklist takes the place of hearing his voice. Martha was busy with her list while Jesus was speaking right in the next room. Your time is better spent first sitting at his feet.

Filter the Noise

Because words of all different kinds meet your ears every day, you need a filter. Filters catch things that shouldn't go any further. Filters on your water faucet, in your HVAC unit, or in your pool stop impurities, dirt, or objects from getting through. Filters only let circulate whatever the system is built for—whatever is healthy for it. You need a filter for all the words you hear. Some of it is just noise. Not everything should be allowed to circulate in your heart and mind. The question to use as a filter is, **Do these words bring life?**

A quick scroll of Instagram will show you that's not as easy to answer as it sounds. A variety of good-sounding messages, mindsets, and ideologies are pushed at you all the time. Every day I see words like you deserve more opportunities; this is your sign that it's time to chase that dream; you are exactly where you need to be; if it's still on your mind, it's worth taking the risk; only surround yourself with people who make you feel empowered, informed, and inspired; and God is going to do something amazing in your life today.

But is a nagging thought really a good way to make a decision? Is now really the right time for that dream? Which of these are words of life for you? How do you know if the messages are good? Timely? What about just *true*? How do you decide which words are the noise you filter? It's easy to be blown back and forth as our thoughts and emotions react to the words we see and hear. There are better words: the Word of God. If heard on a regular basis, God's Word will catch whatever you're hearing that won't lead you down the right path.

My daughters were in the car with me, and the older one played a country song that was popular with a few of her friends. It was a pretty typical country song about heartbreak and a man who needs whiskey glasses to make it through the pain. I spent part of my childhood in Nashville, so I've heard a lot of country music. I didn't think much of it, but when the song was over, my younger daughter spoke up from the back seat. She said, "I don't like that song, Mom. It's not what you told us. I don't think God wants us using alcohol to solve problems." Her sister gave me a huge eye roll, and I laughed. It seemed like an overly serious reaction to a lightweight country song, but then I realized how delighted I was with her response! She *heard* the words and had a filter for what she was hearing. She rejected the message because it didn't match up with what she understood as the way toward truth and life.

My daughter went through an evaluation process that was almost unconscious. Hers took a minute or two. Sometimes all you need is just a moment of pause with a God-formed conscience. Sometimes filtering happens as you turn something over in your mind for a day or two while considering Scripture or praying. Other times you might need a meeting with a trusted friend for advice or some professional counseling to untangle your heart. Been there! You can use the Word of God, alive both in the Scriptures and in the body of Christ, to help filter out noise that won't lead you to the goodness and abundance of a life in the kingdom of God. I praised my daughter for doing exactly what I wanted her to do: hear the words. Consider them carefully and reject anything that isn't consistent with the life God wants for you—a life Jesus lived and taught about when he was here.

Cows do this well. That's right. Cows. You need to hear like a cow eats. Cows ingest a *huge* amount of food—about as much as the number of words you're going to hear today. They swallow a whole bunch of everything and then decide what to keep chewing. Cows actually have four stomachs! The first stomach is a sort of storage bin that's about the size of a large trash can. Its job is to hold all the food until the cow can start to sort it and chew it. You're not going to be able to stop yourself from taking in *all* the words coming at you today, but you don't have to swallow and digest them all. Some are not going to nourish you and bring you life, some are inconsequential background din, and some need to be totally filtered out.

Cows aren't afraid to just spit stuff out. As cows chew, they instinctively spit to the side anything that won't nourish them—sticks, rocks, bad grass, trash, whatever. You can spit out the trash too. If your friend's social media post doesn't match the words of Jesus about money or sex or marriage or prayer or forgiveness or whatever else—spit it out. If words you hear lure you into a bad habit again? Spit them out. If they cause bitterness or anger to multiply in your heart? Spit them out. How about that thing your mom said you were that doesn't match God's words about you? Spit it out. Got words of worry that run on repeat, causing you to live in fear? Spit them out. Hear yourself accuse God of being something that doesn't line up with who the Bible says he is? Spit it out. Whatever gets caught in the filter of the Word isn't going to bring you any life. Life is found only in words that can pass through the filter of the attitudes, actions, and authority of the Word of God. As you spend time hearing the Bible more deeply, your filter gets better and stronger, and you live your life surrounded by quality words circulating through your systems, keeping you healthy and growing.

The filter you set will determine which words you keep and which words fade away, which words you listen to as quality sounds and which words are just noise, which words lead to death and which words lead to life. Jesus said, "The words I have spoken to you—they are full of the Spirit and life" (John 6:63). The words *he* has spoken lead to life. Only the Word of God can sift through all the noise. Life is loud. If you turn down the volume of the stadium and hum around you and turn up the volume of the Word of God, you're going to find yourself standing on much more solid ground.

6

HAVE A PLAN

To turn up the volume of the Word of God, you need a plan. You're not going to accidentally hear more of the Bible in your everyday life. Everything important to you has some sort of plan that goes with it: date nights, classes at the gym, a savings account, work hours. I used to run marathons. If there was one thing that my training taught me, it's that faithfulness to your plan over time gets you to the finish line. You cannot cram in more miles in the last few weeks of training. Marathons don't work that way. Your body needs miles and speed and hills little by little to build endurance and adjust to the demands of the race. Your relationship with Jesus through his Word is similar to marathon training. I want you to cross the finish line saying what Paul said about his own life at the end: "I have fought the good fight, I have finished the race, I have kept the faith" (2 Tim. 4:7). I don't want you to get off course or lose hope or hit a mental low point at mile sixteen because you can't imagine having ten more miles to go. You need a plan.

You have a shepherd who has run ahead of you. He's been where you are going and is ready to lead you a mile at a time. He has encouragement for you. He has wisdom about what's just ahead. He knows where the water stops are. He knows your pace and when to push you. He has pretzels and power gels and orange juice planned for you. He knows what you need for a pick-me-up on the hills. He has running partners who will jump in and run with you and sign holders who will cheer you on. He has a map of the porta potties. Very important. There's even a huge celebration planned at the finish line.

Your job? Have a training plan. Run it faithfully. And stay near him. You have to be able to hear his voice.

Constant exposure to his Word will tune your ear. You'll be able to pick it out even when the crowd gets loud, or the music is blasting around you. If you hear it over and over and over again as you train in the quiet, you'll be able to follow when you hear him directing you in the race.

> The sheep listen to his voice. He calls his own sheep by name and leads them out. When he has brought out all his own, he goes on ahead of them, and his sheep follow him because they know his voice. (John 10:3–4)

It's his pleasure and his job to lead you. It's *your* job to stay near the sound of his voice. That's where your plan comes in. Jesus is not always going the direction you might feel or think. He is not always going the way you'd choose. His vision and understanding are far beyond yours. Too many of us grew up in places, churches, or families that never told us about the amazing connection we get to have every day with Jesus through the Spirit. Instead, his voice was reduced to rules about how to be good or what Christians do. I have no interest in bullet points of how good Christians live. What I want is to know a real and living God whose Word shows me the way to life every single day. In my real life! You'll learn the sound, tone, and language he speaks. And for that, a training plan helps.

Throughout the Bible, God often said to his own people through the prophets, "Return to me" (see Isa. 44; Jer. 3; Joel 2; Zech. 1; Mal. 3). People have always had a tendency to wander off course, to follow other voices. Through prophets like Isaiah, God called his people back to hear and follow his Word so they could get the specific direction and learning that only God has. Our generation is no different. We have a tendency to wander away too.

> Listen and hear my voice;
> pay attention and hear what I say.
> When a farmer plows for planting, does he plow
> continually?
> Does he keep on breaking up and working the soil?
> When he has leveled the surface,
> does he not sow caraway and scatter cumin?
> Does he not plant wheat in its place,
> barley in its plot,
> and spelt in its field?
> His God instructs him
> and teaches him the right way. . . .
> All this also comes from the LORD Almighty,
> whose plan is wonderful,
> whose wisdom is magnificent.
>
> (Isa. 28:23–29)

You can hear God speak more often, instructing and teaching you properly, showing you when and how to plow, plant, and harvest in just the right way. The Holy Spirit has wonderful counsel and great wisdom for you. Reading the Bible to hear God's words regularly will allow you to receive so much more of the Spirit's counsel. Meeting with God is your privileged connection to him in Christ, and I want you to take full advantage!

Don't shy away from a plan because you only have a small pocket of time to offer at first. Remember your plan to show up? Whatever you defined a few chapters ago, the Word of God can be heard in that space. Bring Jesus what you have. He does miracles when we offer in earnest whatever we have to give, like he did one day with his disciples. The disciples didn't have much to offer. They weren't trying to shortchange Jesus or give him their scraps; they just didn't think what they had was worth much. Jesus asked them to bring it to him anyway. With it, he fed not only them but also thousands of others.

> "We have here only five loaves of bread and two fish," they answered.
> "Bring them here to me," he said. And he directed the people to sit down on the grass. Taking the five loaves and the two fish and looking up to heaven, he gave thanks and broke the loaves. Then he gave them to the disciples, and the disciples gave them to the people. They all ate and were satisfied, and the disciples picked up twelve basketfuls of broken pieces that were left over. (Matt. 14:17–20)

You'll be amazed at how a simple plan to read the Bible will multiply the Word in your life. I'm big on having a specific plan to read the Bible that outlines your readings from four to seven days per week. You can get these outlines from so many places. There are apps, books, websites, email plans, and devotionals. I've seen excellent versions of all these methods. I'll offer you one right now, just in case it's the right moment for you to begin. No excuses! Here's a simple plan for the next four months that will introduce you to key parts of Scripture beginning with what the whole story points to: Jesus. It offers a sample of genres and gives you the win of getting through a few whole books. No need to look further if you don't want to.

YOUR READING PLAN

Month 1	
John 1–21	Start with "Who was Jesus?"
Month 2	
Psalm 1–5;	Practice praying with Scripture a little.
Genesis 1–15	Go back to the very beginning of the story.
Month 3	
Genesis 16–39	Read the patriarchs and foundations of your faith.
Month 4	
Genesis 40–50; Jonah 1–4; Ephesians 1–6; Ruth 1–4	Read other genres of the Bible: prophet, letter, historical.

Hearing the Word is the secret to a thriving connection to God. A plan might not sound fun or sexy or even particularly spiritual, but it's critical to you getting to know the Holy Spirit and his tone of voice, words, language, history, and personality. Getting familiar with him in the pages of the Bible makes for much easier communication when you're *not* sitting with your Bible open. The Holy Spirit knows the path God has set for you. His job is to teach you about the words Jesus spoke and to help you bring them to mind when you're out there running on the course, living your life.

I remember a time when I was on my way to pick up my son from practice, and my mind was racing. I was angry and upset at an email from his teacher I'd gotten earlier that day about some potential plagiarism on an assignment. I can be pretty hard-core when it comes to both honesty and academics, so this pushed all my buttons. On the way, I whispered a prayer, *Lord, help me have the right words.* I knew instinctively that I needed help on this one. A couple minutes later, I was stopped at a red light, and as I pressed the gas again, words popped into my head: grace and truth. Immediately, I recognized these words from John 1:14: "The Word became flesh and made his dwelling among us. We have seen his glory, the glory of the one and only Son, who came from the Father, full of grace and truth." Grace and truth were perfectly combined in the person of Jesus. In a nanosecond I realized that if I wanted to look *anything* like Jesus in the exchange I was about to have, I would need both grace *and* truth. Anything other than that wouldn't be handling my kid with love.

Recognizing those words meant *everything* to how I handled the conversation we had when he got in the car five minutes later. Without a doubt, I would have left out the grace if I hadn't heard those words at the stoplight. From there to the gym entrance of the school, I wrestled with what grace looked like and how to communicate that in equal measure with the truth part that came all too easily. Hearing the words of God right then meant I was able to love my son a little more like Jesus might have. I would have failed without them.

I wonder how many times I have thrown up the generic "help me parent my kids with wisdom" prayer. This was a specific answer to that prayer at a specific moment in time, and it all hinged on me recognizing his Word when it was whispered in my ear. The Word is alive in us if we have the Holy Spirit. It is accessible to us even when we aren't sitting with a Bible in our hand, working our reading plan. But hearing his voice regularly starts right there, with reading and listening to his Word.

When you work your reading plan, there are three core elements to use any time you engage with Scripture. These three things can be done in five to ten minutes or two hours or more! They take you from a *reading plan* to a *meeting plan* where you actually try to connect with God in his Word. You can easily adjust or try some add-ons based on your time, season, and preferences. Experiment and see how much better you begin to hear.

YOUR MEETING PLAN: PRAISE, READ, PRAY

Praise

Focus on God first. You're there to meet with a personal God—not a spiritual force. Praise is really just acknowledging him, his presence, and the truth of who he is. It gets your head right for your time together, taking your eyes off of you and putting them on God. Jesus, too, taught that connection begins with who God is: "Our Father in heaven, hallowed be your name." Yours might sound like "Father, I see the truth about you when I look at the fall colors from my window. You are a God of rhythm, variety, and beauty." Or, "Lord, you are the almighty, powerful, and warrior. I feel powerless, and I'm thankful you're not." Tell him anything true that focuses you on him and his character. If you spend five minutes speaking or writing praise to God about who he is, it will shift your heart and mind for the whole day.

Read

Read a minimum of one paragraph of Scripture from the plan you are following. Then, use these interactions with the Word to help you focus and understand:

- **Observe.** Underline, jot thoughts or notes, draw arrows or pictures of what is described, make lists of repetitive words and similar ideas. Read (or listen) carefully. When you move your body, it somehow helps you make connections and engage. This is why I like a paper Bible and notebook instead of a screen. But you can engage on a device as well.

- **Summarize.** Put the main idea into your own words. This ensures you understand what the text is actually saying and exposes confusion. If you can't do this, don't go any further until you use other resources to help you get to the basic point.

- **Interact.** Write or speak to him what you think and feel about this. Ask questions. Express emotion. Share whatever you want with him about these words.

- **Connect.** Take a few minutes to connect what you read yesterday to today's reading. How are they related? This helps you track the flow of the chapter and book so you don't lose the bigger picture of what's being said. Meaning is determined by context. You've got to keep track of where you are.

- **Anchor.** Identify one verse or phrase you want to take with you. I call this my anchor because it helps me stay connected to the Word throughout the day. This is often what God is saying to me from my reading. Write down your anchor or say it to yourself multiple times before you close your Bible. You'll be amazed at how the Spirit reminds you of it at just the right moment in the day.

Pray

Pray not only for yourself but also for people in your life and your church, country, and world. I often use my key phrase from the reading or a psalm to pray from. Using Scripture to pray keeps you powerfully connected to God's heart and will. Speak out loud. Write in a journal. Or do what I do and use shorthand with God—names and phrases in lists in a journal that I talk more about as I pray. Do it the way that works for you.

YOUR MEETING PLAN: ADD-ONS

The following are other things you can add on before, after, or during the time you praise, read, and pray. These are not a substitute for reading and praying from the Bible, but they can enhance or extend the depth and richness of time you spend with God. I add them based on the leading of the Spirit or my season, day, mood, need, and time.

Deeper study

Studying ideas in Scripture helps make deeper connections in and across the Word of God. The depth, wisdom, and beauty of Scripture become apparent with just a small amount of study. Do any of the following with words, concepts, places, people, or phrases from your reading:

- Read it in various Bible translations (ESV, NIV, NET, NKJV, NASB, NLT, MSG, CEB, etc.).
- Cross-reference where it's found in other parts of the Bible for insight on common context and to make connections across Scripture.
- Look up keywords in the original language for deeper insight and understanding of meaning.
- Read a commentary on the chapter. I might choose this exercise if I am having trouble understanding the overall meaning or the historical context, or if I feel I am missing something.

Follow-up notes

Capture thoughts about your life, relationships, or priorities in follow-up notes to yourself. Maybe you need to consider taking action on something, or you need to text someone, set up a meeting, add something to a to-do list, or share an encouraging word. Capture these somewhere and don't miss the promptings from the Spirit, even if the action comes in a couple hours or days. You think you'll remember, but you won't!

So make notes for yourself on what the Word might look like in action in your life.

Silence

Silence is a reset button. It can be great before you even begin. Set a timer for anywhere from one to ten minutes and literally just sit in silence. I close my eyes sometimes. Other times, I'm outdoors just breathing everything in. Silence connects you back to yourself and to the Spirit of God. It helps you notice what's really going on in your heart, mind, and spirit.

Audio

Listen to the Bible on audio too. Or read it out loud. Listen in your car to whatever you read that day; you will hear different things. It helps me follow the flow of a book better. The writings in the Bible were originally read out loud to groups of people, and the writers wrote with that in mind. You'll hear things you'd have missed if you only used your eyes.

Brain dump

Do this if your mind is overloaded with to-dos or worries, or if you're spinning on one topic you can't let go. Journal or say these thoughts, feelings, or lists out loud and decide to set them aside for the few minutes you have to be with God. Whatever distracts you to this degree is going to steal your focus from the Bible. God wants your attention, so get out whatever's on repeat in your mind, acknowledge it openly, and ask for God's help to give him the rest of your time. If I do this and notice similar words or a theme, I jot them down and make them the focus of study later.

Music

Music can somehow bypass your mind and touch your heart in interesting ways. It also seeds truth and theology without book learning. When I use music as part of my time with God, I choose songs that include the words of Scripture. It feeds me truth and helps it soak in deeper. And (bonus!) the words seem to pop out automatically later on. (Anyone else ever seem to remember the words to some random song you loved in high school? I rest my case. I just wish fewer of mine were from Salt-N-Pepa.)

Memorize Scripture

Sometimes I intentionally memorize verses. Even if I don't remember the exact verse word for word two years later (though I often do!), the bits and pieces come back so much easier at the right time. This is like practicing vocabulary and grammar for the language of the Holy Spirit and arming yourself with the Word for any time you need it.

Read a devotional

A devotional can give the fresh perspective of another believer during your time with God. I use these if I am dry and need a pick-me-up. I only choose ones that encourage me to read a passage of Scripture along with it. I never want to substitute someone else's words for the Bible itself or accidentally give away my time with God in favor of time with another person's words. The Bible is unique among all books. Encouragement in it is great; substitution for it is not.

Surround yourself

Copy key Scripture from your reading and put it up around you in your daily life. Make it your phone background, get a chalkboard in the kitchen, place sticky notes on your bathroom mirror, set reminders on your phone. Surround yourself with the truth you read later in the day and week. If Scripture lives richly in the places you are, it will speak to you at times you don't expect!

As you begin to work your reading plan and turn it into actual times that you meet with God through the pages of the Bible, you will find connections, people, and overarching themes that pop up in more than one book and more than one period of history.

If you're anything like me, it'll pique your curiosity. Why did Jesus talk about Jonah as a sign? Why are the names of the patriarchs of Genesis involved in one of the names for God? Why does Paul write so many letters to Jewish people dealing with these ancient laws of Moses and connecting them to their faith in Christ? You'll start to get a sense that there is actually one big story taking place. And it might just bother you enough to find out what that is.

KNOW THE STORY

Reading the Bible is good, but living its story is even better. If you understand the big picture of God's story—past, present, and future—his voice will begin to resound in your life. You'll begin to truly know him and hear all the ways he's inviting you to become a part of his kingdom. You are invited into a life where the words of the Bible are not disconnected precepts or pieces of history but are fused together into the foundation on which you stand and build every day because you know God himself. The Holy Spirit is going to draw you into a brand-new story. The Bible is *your* story.

A woman said to me recently, "All I wanted to do was read the story of how Jesus was born, and it started with a long list of names I couldn't pronounce. I got bored halfway through and stopped." To her, Matthew 1 was a meaningless list of names. (My best advice on the pronunciation thing is just to make it up and say it with confidence.) I get it; I've been there. However, that long list of boring names was actually put there for a reason. It's evidence that you're reading a bigger story. The book of Matthew was written so that the Jewish nation would know and believe that Jesus was their long-awaited Messiah, promised many generations before to come through one particular family line. *That* family line. Those weird names were put there as an indicator that the readers of this book are about to pick up the next chapter in a bigger story that was previously to be continued.

The Bible Is a Story

The problem with reading the Bible is that the story isn't written entirely in order. Each part assumes you understand all the other parts. Very frustrating sometimes, yes. But amazingly, with sixty-six books, thirty-five(ish) authors, and written over 1,500 years, Scripture actually does tell one story. There are some things to know about how it's put together, and you've got to find a way to make the connections. It takes a while to begin to understand all the interconnected parts. When I started reading the Bible, I thought that would happen magically, that I'd suddenly begin to understand how all the books were connected. Turns out, it doesn't work like that. You actually need to learn the basic events of Scripture and how they form the story of God over time. Most of us who have any experience with the Bible have heard excerpts or chapters in bits and pieces, and only get glimpses of the big picture. I think most people avoid the parts that are harder to understand, but that only means you'll never know the whole story! I did this for years, but it only produced an annoying, sneaking feeling that I was missing something. It grew and grew until one day I bought something online out of sheer frustration.

I ordered a ten-foot-long Bible timeline.

Like you do.

I was tired of not getting it. For about a year, every time I read the Bible, I'd spread this ridiculously big timeline out on my living room floor. Sometimes it would take me twenty-five minutes just to understand the first verse of a book that talked about some king or era or prophet I'd never heard of. I know that doesn't sound fun, but I didn't know a better way to figure it out. Maybe there was one. Maybe not. But it's how I began to learn the past. If I came across a name or an event as I read, I wouldn't go any further until I understood where it fell on the timeline. Things began to unscramble in my mind. In my own stumbling way, I made connections between the history and the books, people, and events of the Bible. I sketched this picture in my own journal to represent this growing understanding that I was getting. I added to it as my understanding grew.

As I learned the story of God's past, I began to hear it a little differently—less like a history lesson and more like a family story taking place over many generations, all pointing to one person: Jesus. Learning the past opened my ears to Jesus all the way through the Scriptures. I picked up on words, themes, and important events in his life that were repeated, foretold, or echoed somewhere else in the Bible. The Bible isn't a series of historical events where God is simply involved to teach some morality and wisdom, but instead, it's one large narrative pointing to a man named Jesus. There was a beginning and a middle of his story, and your life is taking place in one of his later chapters somewhere nearer to the end. If your mind gets a little fuzzy reading about priests' garments or sacrifices in Leviticus and judgments pronounced on the nation of Edom by Obadiah, don't worry. God is going to help you. Even the disciples struggled to connect all the Scriptures to Jesus. A few days after Jesus died, some of them were walking and talking about everything that had gone down with his death on the cross. Needless to say, they were bewildered, struggling to make sense of it all. Jesus suddenly appeared among them, but no one recognized him. He asked what they were talking about, and they answered, "About Jesus of Nazareth . . . a prophet, powerful in word and deed before God and all the people . . . sentenced to death, and . . . crucified" (Luke 24:19–20). The man they thought was the Messiah had been killed, and none

Timeline Key

1. Creation
God creates in light and perfect order, but sin enters the perfect home of the garden of Eden through Adam and Eve, bringing a downward spiral of darkness and rebellion against the Creator.

2. The Patriarchs
God began his plan of redemption from sin when he chose Abraham and made a covenant that his family would become a great nation, live in a specific land, and bring blessing to all people.

3. Slavery in Egypt
Because of famine, the family moved to Egypt for protection through Joseph, who served at the right hand of Pharaoh. They became so numerous there that they were eventually enslaved.

4. The Exodus
God sent Moses with power and miracles to rescue his chosen family from Egypt. They escaped under doorways painted with the blood of a lamb and through a parted sea.

5. The Wilderness
God established a covenant with his people and gave them laws and culture to create a holy nation. They promised to be faithful to it, but failed and spent forty years in the wilderness.

6. Conquest for Promised Land
Before death, Moses called them back to the covenant and to faith. Joshua took Israel (the twelve tribes of Jacob) into battle for possession of the land promised to Abraham, which got split by tribe.

7. The Judges
A series of "judges" were the loose leadership structure among the tribes who fought surrounding enemies together (enmity rooted in Genesis genealogies). Israel was never truly faithful to their covenant and eventually demanded a king.

8. The (United) Kingdom of Israel
Saul was the first king, rejected by God. David then ruled. Though flawed, David was known for his love for the Lord who made a covenant for David's line to rule over an everlasting kingdom. Solomon, his son, ruled next and built a great temple but was ultimately unfaithful.

9. The Divided Kingdoms of Israel and Judah
Israel divided into two kingdoms: Israel (ten tribes, North) and Judah (two tribes, South, tribe of rightful kingship). Despite the calls for repentance of God's prophets, both nations were unfaithful to the covenant, so the terms were fulfilled and enemies destroyed them (Assyria—Israel; Babylon—Judah) along with Jerusalem and the temple.

10. Exile
Israel disappeared, but Judah was exiled into Babylon and a remnant preserved. Exile lasted seventy years—the precise terms of the covenant—during which prophets still spoke of repentance, restoration, and glorious return to the land and the Lord.

11. The Return and Rebuilding
King Cyrus decreed exiles could return, and a small faithful number went to Jerusalem to rebuild the temple under Zerubbabel (line of David) so the presence of God could return to his people. Ezra and Nehemiah led later waves of exiles home to rebuild the culture and city walls.

12. Four Hundred Years between Old and New Testaments
With a small remnant and temple, Israel had no glory or independent rule. Persia, Greece, and eventually Rome ruled. No prophets speak and no Scripture is written during this time of "silence." Prophetic promises of redemption and restoration rest on the promised Messiah.

During this period the Maccabean revolt. Jews cleansed the temple from desecration by a godless ruler, and the festival of Hanukkah was born to commemorate the miracle that occurred.

13. Birth and Ministry of Christ
Jesus was born in fulfillment of messianic prophecies. He kept the Law with no sin, fulfilling the covenant perfectly. Descended from Adam, Abraham, and David and having divine power, he was still rejected as the Christ and put to death on a cross, which ultimately was part of God's providential plan.

14. The Church Age
Jesus was resurrected as the sign that he was the Son of God and Savior for all people. The promises of redemption, restoration, and glory will be realized through him. His Spirit came to the apostles so they could spread his gospel and teach all nations, baptizing in the name of the Father, Son, and Holy Spirit as we await his return.

15. You
God has a family created by faith that you are adopted into through Jesus Christ. While you will ultimately prove unfaithful on your own, his sacrifice created a new covenant by his body and blood to return you to the status of "faithful" in Christ. All who possess the deposit of the Spirit will be one with Christ in his coming return, restoration, and glory where all prophetic promises will be fulfilled and creation restored to an everlasting Eden.

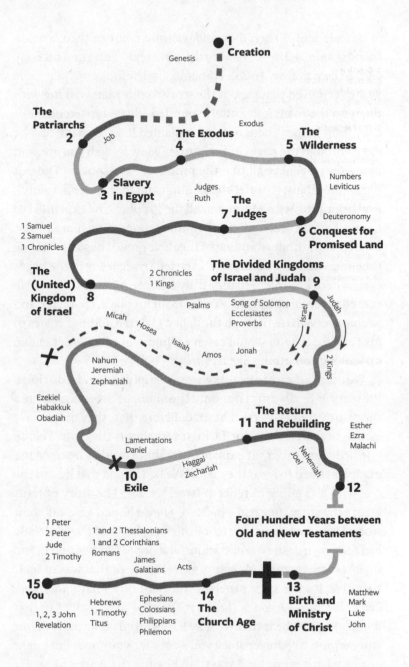

1 Creation
Genesis

The Patriarchs 2
Job

The Exodus 4
Exodus

5 The Wilderness
Numbers
Leviticus

Slavery 3 in Egypt

The 7 Judges
Judges
Ruth

Deuteronomy

6 Conquest for Promised Land

1 Samuel
2 Samuel
1 Chronicles

The (United) Kingdom of Israel 8

2 Chronicles
1 Kings

The Divided Kingdoms of Israel and Judah 9

Psalms

Song of Solomon
Ecclesiastes
Proverbs

Judah

Micah
Hosea
Isaiah
Amos
Jonah

Israel

Nahum
Jeremiah
Zephaniah

2 Kings

Ezekiel
Habakkuk
Obadiah

The Return 11 and Rebuilding

Esther
Ezra
Malachi

Lamentations
Daniel

Haggai
Zechariah

Nehemiah
Joel

10 Exile

12

Four Hundred Years between Old and New Testaments

1 Peter
2 Peter
Jude
2 Timothy

1 and 2 Thessalonians
1 and 2 Corinthians
Romans

James
Galatians

Acts

15 You

Hebrews
1 Timothy
Titus

Ephesians
Colossians
Philippians
Philemon

14 The Church Age

13 Birth and Ministry of Christ

Matthew
Mark
Luke
John

1, 2, 3 John
Revelation

of it made sense. Then they said, weirdly, some of their women friends came back from visiting the grave and "didn't find his body . . . said he was alive" (v. 23). I can imagine the looks on their faces as they reported that part of the story to this man walking with them on the road; it definitely sounded a little far-fetched. But then Jesus helped them out. He explained it all to them, and he did it through the pages of Scripture: "'How foolish you are, and how slow to believe all that the prophets have spoken! Did not the Messiah have to suffer these things and then enter his glory?' And beginning with Moses and all the Prophets, he explained to them what was said in all the Scriptures concerning himself" (vv. 25–27). As my understanding of the Bible grew, I began to see my timeline a little bit differently. I started to see Jesus in the pages everywhere I looked. History truly became *his* story. The Bible started to reveal him and the truth about his plans, character, and people everywhere through the pages. I started adding crosses to my timeline when I would catch a glimpse of him, and it ended up looking something like the image on page 111.

We need our ears to hear as we read Scripture. For the disciples, the story of God wasn't clear until the moment they encountered the resurrected Jesus on that road. Before that, they didn't have ears to hear that a crucified Christ was always the plan. There's one little sentence that explains why they couldn't hear. As the disciples talked to Jesus they said, "We had hoped that he was the one who was going to redeem Israel" (v. 21). The story of Jesus wasn't the story they had expected. They'd hoped for a different story. They weren't looking to join *his* story because they'd already had their own desires, expectations, and hopes for themselves and their nation. A cross? An empty grave? None of that was in their narrative. It's the same problem you and I often have: *they were living their own version of the story.* There's a part of all of us that doesn't want to hear that we may have gotten some parts of our story wrong. Whatever story you wrote for your own life might just be what's preventing you from hearing the voice of Jesus.

I remember printing out my résumé of activities to attach to my college application. I was giving it a last glance as I tore off the dot-matrix printer paper margin down the sides. I was sure the long list of leadership roles, together with my academic performance, was the way into the life I wanted. That was my story, and it had worked for me—until about eighteen months later anyway. In my first semester of college, I was sitting in a huge lecture hall when a friend leaned over and asked if I was okay. I couldn't answer her. My heart was beating like crazy, and the sound of blood was rushing through my ears. I got terribly dizzy, followed by a wave of nausea. I felt like I wasn't fully present for about a minute, and then it passed. This was the first of a handful of these experiences my freshman year. I was living in the same story of achievement and performance through college that I'd lived in high school. The anxiety was a sign that a flood was coming. I felt the ground shifting, but I didn't have a better place to stand.

The day I admired my own résumé, I was writing my own story. The day I got married, I had a story I thought would unfold too. The day I started my corporate career, I was living another chapter of my own. I didn't have ears to hear any other account of my life, and I never once considered that my version didn't have a happy ending. My ears were clogged with a tale that wasn't going to happen. Your old story may be in the way of you stepping into a new one.

Jesus met another woman whose own story hadn't gotten her very far either. He met her at a well in Samaria and challenged the life she'd created for herself because he knew her past.

> "Go, call your husband and come back."
> "I have no husband," she replied.
> Jesus said to her, "You are right when you say you have no husband. The fact is, you have had five husbands, and the man you now have is not your husband." (John 4:16–18)

The Cross

1. Creation
"In the beginning was the Word, and the Word was with God, and the Word was God. He was with God in the beginning. Through him all things were made; without him nothing was made that has been made" (John 1:1–3).

2. The Patriarchs
Jesus was the real descendant of Abraham who brought blessing to the world, and any with faith join the numerous descendents promised to him (Gal. 3:7). Jesus "redeemed us in order that the blessing given to Abraham might come to the Gentiles through Christ Jesus, so that by faith we might receive the promise of the Spirit" (Gal. 3:13–14).

3. Slavery in Egypt
As Jacob's family was physically enslaved in Egypt, humanity is born spiritually enslaved to sin. We need freedom from "the prince of this world" by Jesus, the perfect Moses, who came with miraculous plans and power for an eternal rescue. We, like Israel, will say, "The LORD is my strength and my defense; he has become my salvation" (Exod. 15:2).

4. The Exodus
Jesus was the ultimate Passover Lamb (1 Cor. 5:7), announced by John the Baptist as "the Lamb of God" (John 1:29) and crucified during Passover (Mark 14:12) as the sacrifice for sin and the gateway to freedom from humanity's slavery. He was called by Peter the "lamb without blemish or defect" (1 Pet. 1:19) and exists forever as the Lamb slain for us (Rev. 5:6).

5. The Wilderness
Jesus fulfills the Law given by Moses in the wilderness (Matt. 5:17) which we cannot do on our own. He is the high priest and the perfect sacrifice in a heavenly tabernacle (Heb. 9:11–14) to cleanse us from sin and meet God in his holy place. "For what the law was powerless to do because it was weakened by the flesh, God did by sending his own Son in the likeness of sinful flesh to be a sin offering" (Rom. 8:3).

6. Conquest for Promised Land
Jesus has conquered by his victory on the cross, so by faith we can share in the inheritance that was promised to Abraham. "For this reason Christ is the mediator of a new covenant, that those who are called may receive the promised eternal inheritance" (Heb. 9:15).

7. The Judges
Jesus has the authority to judge: "For as the Father has life in himself, so he has granted the Son also to have life in himself. And he has given him authority to judge because he is the Son of Man" (John 5:26). Jesus offers perfect justice and mercy through the cross. His name is "Faithful and True. With justice he judges and wages war" (Rev. 19:11).

8. The (United) Kingdom of Israel
Jesus is the promised Davidic King on the throne of an everlasting kingdom given to him by his Father. His second coming will usher in the events leading to a final earthly rule into which you are invited to reign with him, "his Son, who as to his earthly life was a descendant of David, and who through the Spirit of holiness was appointed the Son of God in power by his resurrection from the dead: Jesus Christ our Lord" (Rom. 1:3–4).

9. The Divided Kingdoms of Israel and Judah
God calls us to repent from unfaithfulness and disobedience, as he did with these two nations. Jesus is king over a united, eternal kingdom that cannot be shaken or divided (Heb. 12:28).

10. Exile
We deserve to be scattered and exiled from God just as the nation of Israel was. But the prophets announced a people preserved for God, a return to relationship and home with the Lord. Jesus makes reality what the prophets spoke about: a people who are a "light of the world" (Matt. 5:14); his Spirit in a heart means "you yourselves are God's temple" (1 Cor. 3:16), one day fully rebuilt in glory as part of "the Holy City, the new Jerusalem, coming down out of heaven from God, prepared as a bride beautifully dressed for her husband" (Rev. 21:2).

11. The Return and Rebuilding
The cross is the decree that we are allowed to return home. Jesus is the way back. Whatever was lost, destroyed, burned, or broken, the Lord will "repay you for the years the locusts have eaten" (Joel 2:25), and do what he said to Zerubbabel: "Not by might nor by power, but by my Spirit" (Zech. 4:6).

12. Four Hundred Years between Old and New Testaments
No matter how silent or oppressed or overrun God's people seem, no other ruler will ever rule over the King of Kings. His kingdom is always advancing, no matter how silently. In the end, "the Lamb will triumph over them because he is Lord of lords and King of kings—and with him will be his called, chosen and faithful followers" (Rev. 17:14).

13. Birth and Ministry of Christ
Jesus had the pedigree of the long-awaited Messiah. Matthew recorded "the genealogy of Jesus the Messiah the son of David, the son of Abraham," (1:1) and Luke recorded him as "the son of Adam, the son of God" (3:38). We are all born in the family of Adam, headed for death. Through Jesus we can be reborn into the family of God, as Abraham's children by faith. We are baptized and raised to life by his Spirit, alive and ruled in grace by the promised son of David in an eternal kingdom.

14. The Church Age
The church is the body of Jesus Christ operating here on earth. "Just as a body, though one, has many parts, but all its many parts form one body, so it is with Christ. For we were all baptized by one Spirit so as to form one body" (1 Cor. 12:12). "Now to each one the manifestation of the Spirit is given for the common good" (1 Cor. 12:7), so God's image and glory is expressed now here on earth.

15. You (Eph. 2:1–9)
"As for you, you were dead in your transgressions and sins, in which you used to live when you followed the ways of this world and of the ruler of the kingdom of the air, the spirit who is now at work in those who are disobedient. All of us also lived among them at one time, gratifying the cravings of our flesh and following its desires and thoughts. Like the rest, we were by nature deserving of wrath. But because of his great love for us, God, who is rich in mercy, made us alive with Christ even when we were dead in transgressions—it is by grace you have been saved. And God raised us up with Christ and seated us with him in the heavenly realms in Christ Jesus, in order that in the coming ages he might show the incomparable riches of his grace, expressed in his kindness to us in Christ Jesus. For it is by grace you have been saved, through faith—and this is not from yourselves, it is the gift of God—not by works, so that no one can boast. For we are God's handiwork, created in Christ Jesus to do good works, which God prepared in advance for us to do."

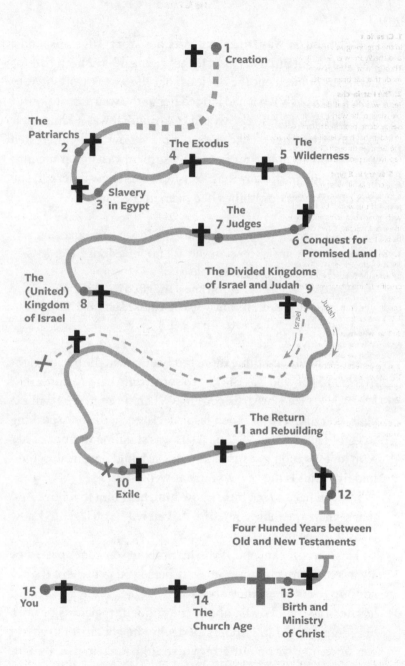

1 Creation

The Patriarchs
2

The Exodus
4

The Wilderness
5

Slavery
3 in Egypt

The
7 Judges

6 Conquest for
Promised Land

The Divided Kingdoms
of Israel and Judah
9

The
(United)
Kingdom
of Israel
8

Israel

Judah

The Return
11 and Rebuilding

10
Exile

12

Four Hunded Years between
Old and New Testaments

15
You

14
The
Church Age

13
Birth and
Ministry
of Christ

Ouch. But it was true. That was her story—five husbands. Any of the potential backstories there must have been bad for her. Jesus pointed out the obvious: her life wasn't working very well. That's likely what had landed her at the well at that time of day; she knew no one else would be around. It was clear in their exchange that she was like many people I know today, interested in what God is doing but not really sure how to fit her life into it. Even though she saw that Jesus was somehow different, she was hung up on how things had been in the past.

> The Samaritan woman said to him, "You are a Jew and I am a Samaritan woman. How can you ask me for a drink?" (For Jews do not associate with Samaritans.)
> Jesus answered her, "If you knew the gift of God and who it is that asks you for a drink, you would have asked him and he would have given you living water." (vv. 9–10)

She wanted something more but overlooked the person right in front of her who was the key to something new. "'I know that Messiah' (called Christ) 'is coming. When he comes, he will explain everything to us.' Then Jesus declared, 'I, the one speaking to you—I am he'" (vv. 25–26). Jesus was standing in front of her with an invitation to a new story. If she could hear it, she could find life. Jesus is the key to yours as well.

But you need to see him, know him, hear him to follow. And that's where the Bible comes in. As you read, you'll get to know Jesus through his past.

This is true for anyone. If you learn about someone's past, they always make much more sense. It helps you get where they're coming from when they speak or act a certain way. When I learned my friend's past about the sudden tragic loss of both her mom and sister, I understood why she got anxious when I was unresponsive on our group text. If I hadn't known, I might have brushed it off or just told her to calm down; but when I understood her past, I knew *her*. I was able to understand her, know her, love her better. When you know someone's story, you know their heart and how it was formed. You can start to anticipate how they'll feel about things. I can't count the number of times I've said things to my kids like, "You know that makes Dad grumpy." Or, "You know how I feel about crumbs right after I've cleaned." (In twenty-four hours I'll have given up again, but they don't dare brush their cracker crumbs on the floor right after I vacuum.)

Knowing someone's story teaches you to see patterns of how that person acts in various situations. When you know the backstory, you understand someone's motives. Over time you start to credit that person with those intentions. You assume that's what they're about because you've witnessed their character. You hear tones and inflections they use when they speak. You recognize catchphrases and slang they like to use. Did you ever notice that friends start to talk like one another? And any mom will tell you they can pick out their own kid's voice in a crowd of kids yelling "Mom!" The same will be true for you and God. As you learn his past through the Scriptures, you'll *know* him better, so you'll be able to tune your ears to his voice.

I believe God speaks in certain ways outside of Scripture, too, revealing parts of his wisdom or will in personal and timely ways through his Spirit. I also think he speaks through his creation in a poetic way that reveals his qualities and puts his truths on display, drawing us toward him. But it's only the Scriptures that tell you who Jesus is. Nothing else explains the history of humanity and God and what Jesus has to do with any of it. To truly live a life connected to God, building what lasts in his kingdom, you need to hear and know God through the life of his Son. We have the Scriptures so we can get to know God's full story, and that will always lead us to Jesus. The words of Jesus bring the whole story together. When you read, the Holy Spirit will be at work alongside you, pushing you toward the resources you need to hear it—even if that's a ten-foot-long timeline. The prayer you can pray as you go is, "**Father, help me see Jesus in this.**"

He will answer this prayer because he wants you to be part of it. God's heart for you is to join his story, and you only fit into it *through Jesus.*

The Bible Is *Your* Story

As I began my long, slow march to understanding the Bible with timelines and charts, I picked up on a theme about temples. This theme was my first lesson in exactly what it means to find the story I was made to live through Christ. All through the Bible there's talk of temples. The first temple was built to house the presence of God with his people. (Like, literally, that's where God resided among his people.) And the nation of Israel brought continual sacrifices there to deal with their sin so they could approach God for an ongoing relationship.

The temple story started in the Old Testament. At first, I simply noted on the timeline when the first temporary temple was built: it was called a tabernacle and was built during the period God's people were on the move so they needed something they could set up and tear down as they went (see Exod. 25). Once they were in a permanent spot, King Solomon built a huge, beautiful temple. Scripture includes all the details about this one, beginning in Exodus 26–31. You will read more than you ever wanted to know about curtains of blue, scarlet, and purple linen flanked by gold cherubim and the linen for the priestly garments. I'm sure you've read passages like this and thought, *What in the world does this have to do with my life? Why do I need to know this?* Once they were in a permanent spot, King Solomon built the first permanent temple (see 1 Kings 5–6). It was planned for, lavishly built, and dedicated in great splendor (see 1 Kings 8).

Next, I noted on my timeline that the first temple was destroyed when Jerusalem was conquered by Babylon (see 2 Kings 25). That was a big deal; the presence of God now had nowhere to live among his people. After that, I made notes about the second temple—the one that was rebuilt through books like Ezra, Nehemiah, Haggai, and Zechariah after the Babylonian captivity ended and some of the Jewish people went back to Jerusalem to live. This was also a really big deal. Now worship and sacrifices could resume, dealing with sin in the nation, and God could be back with his people again. It was this second temple that was eventually renovated and still standing when Jesus was alive (see Ezra 3).

And that's when the temple story got *real* interesting. Jesus was constantly at the temple. I picked up the theme and the importance he seemed to place on it. One day Jesus got really angry at people buying and selling things in the temple courts. He drove them out with a whip and called it his "Father's house" (John 2:16).

The Jewish leaders wanted some sort of verification of his authority to do and say these things. His answer? "Destroy this temple, and I will raise it again in three days" (v. 19). They thought he was crazy. They knew the time it took to build the first and second temples, recorded in 1 Kings, 2 Chronicles, Ezra, and Haggai. They knew that three days was nonsense! So they said, "It has taken forty-six years to build this temple, and you are going to raise it in three days?" (v. 20).

They couldn't hear his story. They were stuck on the past. They didn't have ears to hear where the kingdom of God was going. They only knew what their eyes could see. They weren't a part of the story Jesus was living. John explained what Jesus actually meant: "But the temple he had spoken of was his body" (v. 21). It was Jesus's *body* that would die and be raised in three days. Jesus's body was some sort of temple. And when he did die, Matthew, Mark, and Luke all record at that very moment, "The curtain of the temple was torn in two from top to bottom" (Mark 15:38).

This strange detail recorded when Jesus died on the cross is where this temple story finds meaning for you and me. The story will always bring you to Jesus. The tearing of the curtain of the temple was a symbol that the presence of God is now out from behind the curtain! (The big, thick, linen embroidered one that you read all about!) The death of Jesus paid the price for sin, so the sacrifices can stop! The presence of God is no longer confined to a specific place! We are no longer separated from him because of our sin. Jesus made the final sacrifice; he tore down the temple! And then he rose again three days later in the body of Jesus Christ. Paul explained what it means for every one of us who is now in Christ:

> Don't you know that you yourselves are God's temple and that God's Spirit dwells in your midst? If anyone destroys God's temple, God will destroy that person; for God's temple is sacred, and you together are that temple. (1 Cor. 3:16–17)

You are the sacred place. You are a temple of God himself through the deposit of his Spirit in you. You are part of the body that was raised from the grave. Christ in *you* brings the presence of God everywhere you go. You never need to feel separated from God because of your sin. This is exactly what Jesus told the woman at the well when she questioned him about the temple and who could go to it. Jesus answered her, "Yet a time is coming and has now come when the true worshipers will worship the Father in the Spirit and in truth" (John 4:23). It is the Spirit of God within you that makes you a worshiper, not your presence in a building. Not your continual sacrifices. Jesus tore all that down and made a way for you to worship God every day, anywhere.

The temple story is the story of Jesus, and it is your story too. It isn't just a boring part of the Old Testament. It is an amazing part of *your* story! If you just read 1 Kings 6–7 as boring temple facts and history, then you'll never know that *you* are worth the same time and beauty and expense as Solomon's temple. *You* are worth the same level of planning and time and effort and treasure. God has put all of that into *you* as a place of his very presence.

You might read the book of Lamentations about Jeremiah's cries when he watched the first temple get destroyed by Babylon as just a piece of history. But if you connect that story to yourself through Jesus, then you will hear the wisdom and the warning about how painful life is without the presence of God.

The temple story is about as personal as it gets. It even goes so far as to touch on your sex life in 1 Corinthians 6:18–20:

> Flee from sexual immorality. All other sins a person commits are outside the body, but whoever sins sexually, sins against their own body. Do you not know that your bodies are temples of the Holy Spirit, who is in you, whom you have received from God? You are not your own; you were bought at a price. Therefore honor God with your bodies.

The temple is kept pure and holy for the presence of God.

The story of the temple is deeply personal to you. Boring details and all. If you hear the story of the temple in the Bible, then you will hear who *you* are as a follower of Christ. You will hear how much you are worth, how to care for yourself, who's welcome with you and who's not, why holiness is necessary, and your privilege in having a direct, ongoing relationship with God anytime, anyplace. This seemingly random, boring temple story may have started *way* back in the pages of Scripture but the end of that story now lives in you.

And the temple is just one tiny little part. There's so much more of your story to know.

The Bible is actually your story, and *Jesus* is your way in. Learn your story. Hear his voice. And when you do, put it into practice. You will end up living a vibrant life in the kingdom of God on a firm foundation.

Oh—and God's story isn't over. The next rhythm depends on you. So let's go practice.

PART 3
PRACTICE

At bedtime my daughter often asks me what she should wear to school the next day. I usually ask Siri what the forecast is and then suggest something that she is definitely not going to wear. We go through this little charade multiple nights a week. Every now and then I happen to pick something she was already thinking about wearing, so I feel victorious, but most of the time she ignores me completely and comes downstairs the next morning wearing whatever she was planning to wear in the first place.

I only make suggestions because *she asked*! Sigh. Teenagers.

We do this with God all the time. We come and hear his words, only to do exactly what we were going to do anyway. The day Jesus spoke the parable of the wise and foolish builders, he got in the crowd's face and asked them, "Why do you call me, 'Lord, Lord,' and do not do what I say?" (Luke 6:46).

The title "Lord" suggested a level of reverence and obedience, but Jesus insinuated that he was Lord in name only. People weren't *doing* anything after hearing God's instructions, commands, and truth. They preferred the way they were already doing things. The parable of the wise and foolish builder was his warning about what happens when that's the case. Actually *doing* what Jesus says is where the rubber meets the road. Coming and hearing isn't far enough. We have to put the words into practice.

> Why do you call me, "Lord, Lord," and do not do what I say? As for everyone who comes to me and hears my words and **puts them into practice**, I will show you what they are like. They are like a man building a house, who dug down deep and laid the foundation on rock. When a flood came, the torrent struck that house but could not shake it, because it was well built. But the one who hears my words and **does not put them into practice** is like a man who built a house on the ground without a foundation. The moment the torrent struck that house, it collapsed and its destruction was complete." (Luke 6:46–49, emphasis mine)

The final rhythm of a well-built life is *practice.* Practicing isn't simply about action; it's about obedience. Both builders in the parable built something, but only the one who built on the words of Christ was actually sitting on a foundation. A house that lasts isn't just built by hard work; it's built on actions of obedience to a lord. Without the practice of acting on what you hear, your house will be a house of cards. The good news, however, is that if you're truly *coming* and truly *hearing*, then the last rhythm of *practicing* is almost certain to naturally follow. The doing of the Word is the evidence that the first two rhythms genuinely took root.

In the parable, Jesus reveals why most of the people in the crowd that day were calling him Lord but not doing anything: they hadn't first come to him! There's a connection to the first and last rhythms. A genuine, open heart coming to God is the power that sets all three of these rhythms in motion. People who then hear the Word of God will always be compelled toward action because the Word of God is alive and active. The Spirit's work in our life is magnetic. If your heart is open and you *come* and *hear*, it will become harder and harder to **not** *put into practice* what he says. The impact of the Spirit's words is like a giant magnet pulling you in the direction of obedience—because it's only in alignment with God's commands that you find the life you're searching for. Jesus speaks words that, when obeyed, lead us to life. "I know that his command leads to eternal life. So whatever I say is just what the Father has told me to say" (John 12:50).

The words of Jesus are meant to be obeyed because they will always lead you to life. When you experience the life of God, it ruins you for any substitute. Nothing else will do. You will want to come back and hear more. You will want to keep practicing them in your life. You will want to keep digging until you get to the rock.

I remember being in church as a kid and drawing on the offering envelopes, trying to keep myself still and quiet while the readings and the preaching happened. Even as a young child, I could feel the gravity of the words I was hearing. I knew we were all there in our Sunday best because they were somehow important. Most of Jesus's listeners were Jewish people who felt the same. They had great respect for the words of the prophet Isaiah or Moses—and now Jesus. They *had* the Word of God. They *respected* the Word of God. They just didn't *do* the Word of God. Putting the words into action is the separation between the man who had a foundation and the one who did not. Obedience firms up the ground under your feet for the day the flood comes. It's the evidence of real faith.

Jesus got pretty hard-core about what happens if we don't put his words into action. I kind of wish he hadn't gone all the way to complete destruction in this parable. Whenever someone talks in such dramatic language, I always want to tell them to calm down—that it can't be all that bad. Jesus was trying to shake a crowd who likely felt exactly like that. They were doing things. They were decent folk. They were in the synagogues. And here's

Jesus telling them if they never actually do what he says, then it's over for them. A lack of action indicates a dead faith. A dead faith means you're not just in trouble in this life, you're in much bigger trouble for the one that comes later. Not just a collapse now, but complete destruction. Wow.

I've been in the hearing-only danger zone. I really love the Bible because I connect deeply with God through his Word. I love learning, so I actually enjoy geeking out and hearing all there is to hear. In the end, however, the words are always much easier read than done. You could spend a lifetime listening to the words of Jesus (and I think you should!), but unless the cycle finishes in practice, collapse is still coming. The problem is the sand can hold you up for a good long time. It's packed and hard and it can be just fine for building during long seasons of life. Wherever and whenever it's summertime for you—wherever you're comfortable and safe and successful today—digging down through the hard, dry sand will feel unnecessary and like a waste of time. You're so tempted to think *everything's fine*! And it is.

Until it's not.

Wherever it's summer in your life might be the very place you're in the most danger of skipping the practice and work it takes to lay a strong foundation. That's why the collapse is so surprising when it comes. When I first got married, I misinterpreted my husband's and my compatibility, our excitement about the future, and our good financial picture as signs that we were standing on rock. We weren't. It was summer, so the sand felt fine for building a life on those things. When everything is fine, it's easy to convince yourself these are signs of strength. Nope. The water will rise at some point, and a good job won't save you. Trust me. Instead of arranging better circumstances, you need to ask yourself one question: *When's the last time I did something because of the Word of God?*

It's time to look down and notice what you're standing on.

I'm pro having good jobs. I'm pro listening to sermons and podcasts. I'm pro fun dates and compatibility. I'm pro savings accounts. I'm pro going to church. There's a lot of everyday wisdom for life in doing these things and many others. I'm certainly pro reading your Bible. But I didn't build the immovable core of my faith while I was sitting in a seat doing any of those things. I built them on the move. None of these things will ever in and of themselves build authentic and personal trust in Jesus. My living, breathing, risky experiences with Jesus have formed rock under my feet. It was built when I actually did something he said. When you live out the truth of his words, they will not be blown away or broken down with the next whim or criticism or storm because you've seen it with your own eyes. You've done it with your own body. You've lived it in your own relationships. Christianity is not ultimately about the written words, as important as they are. It's about the Spirit in you compelling you to bring those words to life right here, right now as you follow him. You have to practice today, or there will be no foundation tomorrow.

I like the word *practice* instead of saying "obey" or even simply "do it." *Practice* is a word that relieves any pressure in having to get it right all the time. Practice tells me that imperfect experimentation is welcome—which is great because that's all I've ever done. I've met super-spiritual types who proclaim they won't move a muscle until they are 110 percent sure it's God and 100 percent sure they're going the right way. That's not what Jesus is looking for. Practice feels much closer to the gracious heart of Jesus. Getting it wrong while you try to follow him won't please him any less. His desire is that you would trust him today, and that trust would ground you for whatever you face tomorrow. There's no substitute for discovering that Jesus actually knows what he's talking about! You can find *that* out whether you get it right or get it wrong! But that cannot happen if you never move. Finishing these three rhythms in succession—come, hear, practice—will not only form rock at the foundation of your life but you'll experience the joy and adventure of getting to know a living God.

Don't waste time trying to get it all right. God is delighted with your best attempts to move on his Word. So, c'mon. Let's have a little fun. Let's mess it up a little. Let's go practice together. But you don't have to do it like me; you get to do it like *you* as you experiment and discover that his Word is always good. He is always for you. His words always lead to life. And he is always weaving everything—I mean *everything*—together for your good.

My husband and I have a line we say when we're just going to have to go with it and see what happens. One of us will look at the other, wink, and say, "Only one way to find out!"

If you want to know whether God is real, whether his strength will hold you, whether his words are true, whether there's more good for you, whether you can ever rebuild from the crash you just had, there's *only one way to find out!*

Let's go practice.

8

EXPERIMENT

Oh my goodness, this is the fun part. And the terrifying part. And, sometimes, the agonizing or frustrating part. The moments you practice are the moments you come alive—when you stop believing *in* Jesus and you try just *believing him* instead.

For a year or so, I led a group of women who wanted to grow as followers of Jesus. We did a couple weeks in a deep dive on prayer and fasting. All of us were amateurs when it came to fasting, so I suggested an experiment. We'd seen clearly in the Bible that fasting often accompanied prayers and petitions to God. In a previous meeting, one of the women in our group had shared her twelve-year-long struggle with infertility that had no medical explanation. She was heartbroken. I knew the darkness of infertility struggles, so my heart hurt for her. I proposed we try what we see in Scripture: petition God for her with fasting and prayer. We called it a relay fast and each took twenty-four hours, passing the proverbial baton to the next woman. There were seven of us, so we prayed and fasted on our friend's behalf for a full week. When we met again, we shared our encouragement and prayers with her and discussed the experience. She was grateful, and we felt we'd grown as a result. Then we moved on.

Six weeks later she brought us her positive pregnancy test.

I think I screamed for a full three minutes straight! And then off and on for another hour! We screamed with happiness for her. We screamed because her wait was over. But I screamed for another reason too. That peed-on stick was evidence that God's Word is true. It was evidence of our connection. It was evidence of his power and goodness available to all of us. There will now never be any doubt in his Word that fasting is a means to significant spiritual breakthrough. I might still struggle with my flesh about wanting to do it, but this was scream-worthy evidence that God isn't messing around. He means what he says.

For days after, though, I felt uncomfortable. I had to admit to myself the depth to which I didn't really expect anything to happen—despite what I'd already read in the Bible. I'd have told you I believed that fasting impacts an invisible reality and breaks strongholds. I'd have told you fasting matters in prayer to God. But until that day, I guess I really didn't believe it. Now, I own it. I can never unknow, unsee, and unhear what went down that day. That moment is forever part of the foundation I stand on. All week I kept smiling in amazement. How could God let a bunch of nobodies, who only had enough trust in his words to launch an experiment, use their tiny faith to bring a huge breakthrough that changed someone's life? How amazing that he offers this to all of us!

God loves our pathetic experiments.

Don't Wait for Certain

Practicing the Word of God means launching all kinds of imperfect experiments to see if we can trust in his Word. Practicing means it's okay to be a little rough around the edges with a lot to learn. Practicing is just asking the question, What would it look like to trust God with this? And then doing that. You don't even need an answer you feel sure of—or even a God you feel sure of. Living a life of faith doesn't mean an absence of doubt or fear; it just means you practice anyway. You practice when you're not certain. You move with whatever you can muster in the face of your doubts. We all have a mixture of both, and a little doubt shouldn't stop you from experimenting with the words of Jesus. Even Peter, one of Jesus's closest friends, struggled with doubts. One night Peter and the disciples were out in a boat on the Sea of Galilee, and Jesus came walking out to them on the water. They were terrified. They doubted their own eyes even when Jesus identified himself, but Peter wanted to try out the words of Jesus and see if they held him up.

> "Lord, if it's you," Peter replied, "tell me to come to you on the water."
> "Come," he said.
> Then Peter got down out of the boat, walked on the water and came toward Jesus. But when he saw the wind, he was afraid and, beginning to sink, cried out, "Lord, save me!"
> Immediately Jesus reached out his hand and caught him. "You of little faith," he said, "why did you doubt?" (Matt. 14:28–31)

Peter wasn't even sure it was Jesus. He must have considered the possibility that he was going to sink. But he was willing to do an experiment! He heard Jesus invite him out on the water, and he didn't let his doubt stop him from stepping out of the boat to find out if it was true. Not all doubt. Not all faith. Somewhere in the middle. He had to have felt great about his experiment on those first few steps. He did it! But practice isn't perfect, and his doubt overtook him again. Even then, Jesus was right by his side. Peter wasn't sure and he wasn't ready, but it's always a good time for an experiment.

Sometimes I hear the words of Jesus wrong because I'm clouded by my own imperfections, busyness, insecurities, or my own desires—like the time I was heading to Colorado and asked God to help get me a pair of new boots. It was a hiking boot I needed for part of my trip, and I had asked God if he could help get them to me in time. Amazon said otherwise, but I think my God is bigger than Amazon. I know his Word about being a dad who knows me and likes to give his children good gifts. I wondered if that included cute hiking boots. Why not experiment? So I asked him to help just because I believed he could.

I tracked the delivery of my boots on the app, and it wasn't looking good. I kept asking God anyway. Yes, I felt a little silly, but I also believed I serve a Lord who can do anything he wants, anytime he wants, in any way he wants, including the miraculous delivery of boots. I also thought he cared about me. So I waited as long as I could and then had to leave for the airport. I was bummed to leave without them; I really thought he could and might do it!

On my way out of my neighborhood, I passed an Amazon delivery truck coming in.

I just knew it—those were my boots! I had to decide right then if I was going to practice: was I going to turn the car around or not? Waiting was one thing, but would I believe enough to follow that truck back to my house?

Yes. Yes, I would. I turned around and followed, very stalker-like. I was sure God was delivering them early in response to my prayers. I thought the Spirit had encouraged me to believe God was sending them, so I followed the truck as he turned onto my street. He slowed down as he came to my house! And then I watched the guy get out, grab a box, and drop a package on my next-door neighbor's porch.

Not my boots.

Welp. Guess I needed more practice.

It's likely I just heard my own desires. I mean, I am a girl who loves boots. Maybe I convinced myself God did too. I laughed and went to the airport with plan B in my bag. I'm sure it won't be the last time I get it wrong.

But what if I *hadn't* turned the car around? What was God thinking as he watched me decide? How did it make him feel to see that I believed in his power and ability? If I hadn't turned the car around, I would have missed the chance to experience something with God—even though I was wrong. What did the experiment cost me? Ten minutes and some pride? Not much for the payoff of his delight that I felt. He saw evidence in action that I believed he could and would do something small just because he loves me. I got the boots wrong, but I got that part right.

There's a joy that comes when you practice the Word of God. Whether it all turns out right, that joy is from a Father who is pleased with authentic attempts to respond to his words. Hebrews 11:6 says, "And without faith it is impossible to please God, because anyone who comes to him must believe that he exists and that he rewards those who earnestly seek him." Even imperfect practice creates a relationship with God. It shows him your belief in his presence, his heart, and his character. In Christ, you are standing in the grace to get it wrong! So you can just enjoy the process of growing and connecting and risking to build a life on him.

Don't Wait for the Whole Picture

Practice really is a process, so you can't wait for the whole picture to be revealed. As you listen to the Word of God, it'll probably be just one small thing you can obey. When you do, it tends to reveal the move you need to make after that. God sees exactly where it will take you, but you're on more of a need-to-know basis—and usually you only need one word to practice at a time. So don't wait. If you want the whole picture to be revealed, you'll never move at all.

I volunteered at a prayer night with my church, and a young woman sat down to receive prayer from my friend and me. As we listened to her talk about the prayer she was requesting, I couldn't get out of my head the picture of fluffy pink cotton candy that was spun up on a paper cone. I silently asked God multiple times if he would tell me more, but no response. There's no cotton candy in the Bible, so I was clueless. I couldn't shake the image, so before she got up, I just had to say something. I blurted out, "Do you like cotton candy?"

She stopped cold and looked up at me with wide eyes and said, "What did you just say?" I repeated the question, and she looked stunned when she said, "I love cotton candy! I love it so much that my husband and my friends just went together to buy a cotton candy machine for my basement so I could have some anytime I want!"

What?

We were both in awe. But more importantly, it was only as she answered me that the next words came to my mind from Psalm 139. I spoke from them as I told her, "God knows you! He knows every little tiny thing about you because he's the one who formed you in your mother's womb. He planned every little quirk that makes you, you. And he loves what he made. Even the things that you think are the most insignificant, like your love of cotton candy, he knows and loves about you!"

She cried. I cried. We were both changed by the Word of God that night. The actual words—the fuller understanding—came only *after* I asked about that first random picture of cotton candy. I had to open my mouth. I had to move. I had to do something before it led to more for both of us. That's the only reason any rock formed under my feet that evening. That's why it's now part of my foundation. I was in a real exchange with the Word of God. If I'd known where it was all going, it wouldn't have grown my faith at all.

An early follower of Jesus named Philip knew not to wait for the whole picture. He got one small direction from the Lord one day: "Now an angel of the Lord said to Philip, 'Go south to the road—the desert road—that goes down from Jerusalem to Gaza'" (Acts 8:26).

That's it. No instructions about what to do. Nothing more said. No Bible verse.

And he went.

Once he was on the road, he got the next direction: "The Spirit told Philip, 'Go to that chariot and stay near it'" (v. 29).

So he did.

No instructions about what to do. Nothing more said. No Bible verse.

Once he was beside the chariot, this is what went down: "Then Philip ran up to the chariot and heard the man reading Isaiah the prophet" (v. 30).

Now things get interesting. Philip obeyed one step at a time, and it led him to a guy reading Isaiah. This was certainly not a coincidence, but there were still no more instructions. As he listened, Philip heard the man reading what he knew was a section of Scripture about the Messiah. I can't help but feel that this was his cotton candy moment, because Philip just blurted out, "Do you understand what you are reading?" (v. 30).

And the rest went on from there. It probably wouldn't have mattered what Philip said right then—*anything* that moved things forward, *anything* that indicated he believed this was all God, *anything* that showed his faith in God's ability to keep leading him in this situation. Philip climbed up in the chariot and ended up leading this guy to faith in Jesus as his Savior and baptizing him on the side of the road. Philip didn't wait for the whole picture; he followed step-by-step and took a chance to get to the end of the story.

Don't Wait Until You're Stronger

We tend to want to see the whole story because we want to make sure we are strong enough or prepared for what's coming. But when we wait to get stronger before we act on the words of God, strength never grows because *practice* is the only thing that builds it.

Jesus pushed his followers into situations he knew they weren't strong enough for, like the day they looked at a crowd of thousands and thousands of people and Jesus baffled them by saying, "You give them something to eat."

What?! They said back, "We have only five loaves of bread and two fish—unless we go and buy food for all this crowd" (Luke 9:13). They had to have felt confused, helpless, weak, incapable to do what Jesus asked, but Jesus barely acknowledged that they felt unequal to the task. He already knew they weren't strong enough. That was the whole point.

His answer instead was this:

> "Have them sit down in groups of about fifty each." The disciples did so, and everyone sat down. Taking the five loaves and the two fish and looking up to heaven, he gave thanks and broke them. Then he gave them to the disciples to distribute to the people. They all ate and were satisfied, and the disciples picked up twelve basketfuls of broken pieces that were left over. (vv. 14–17)

Jesus had them organize the people into groups. Can you imagine their conversation? It was probably something like, "Why in the world is he having us do this?" He knew they were unsure of what was happening. He didn't tell them what he was going to do. He knew they felt they didn't have enough, so the whole point was to put their hands on the bread.

Jesus wanted them holding that bread when it multiplied right in their hands. The disciples had no idea the kind of power they were dealing with, and Jesus wanted them to experience it. He wanted them to practice using it. If they were going to live lives standing on him, then they had to experience and expect and count on the resources of the very kingdom of God to be at their disposal. Jesus wanted his disciples to live according to the truth of his Word instead of by the five loaves and two fish they could see in front of them. He pushed them right into an experiment so they could practice it themselves. And then they picked up twelve baskets leftover.

Living inside the truth and power of the kingdom of God takes practice. You've relied on your other set of ears and eyes for a long time. You need to be able to trust the Word of God in the face of your own words that say you need to be more certain or get more information or be stronger before you move. The Word of God invites you to follow him when you're uncertain and weak and can't hear the end—because that's when the rock forms under your feet. It's there that you become convinced of who God is and your foundation gets stronger because it is God himself you are standing on. His power. His confidence. His resources. His forgiveness. His security. His ability.

> For who is God besides the LORD?
> And who is the Rock except our God?
> It is God who arms me with strength
> and keeps my way secure.
>
> (Ps. 18:31–32)

So let's do this. Do it badly. Do it weak. Do it as an imperfect experiment, but start somewhere. He's there. He's good. He's strong enough to hold you up. But there's only one way to find out! Practice.

9

EXPECT RESISTANCE

I was on my way to work, planning for a lunchtime run. It wasn't something I usually did, but that day was perfect for it—glorious weather, a hole in my calendar, and no meetings in the afternoon, which meant a little sweat and a ponytail were no big deal. I was pleased with my little plan. I stopped at a red light just across from my parking lot and watched a woman shuffle across the street in front of me. She caught my eye in the crosswalk because of her odd shuffling, but one glance at the thick white 1980s tube socks shoved into dollar store flip-flops and I understood. She carried a trash bag that probably held everything she owned. As the light turned green, I heard the words "give her your shoes." I glanced over at the brand-new running shoes on my front seat. The words weren't audible, but I heard them loud and clear. I knew right away that it was probably God. I took another look at the shoes and felt resistance rise up in me as I drove into my parking lot. I pushed back out loud, "But, but . . . but I love these shoes. I just got them. I paid a lot for them! And I had a plan for my day!" It all hung on these shoes. I did not want to give them up.

For forty-five seconds, I was in an internal tug-of-war; despite my pushback, I couldn't bring myself to put my car into park. I had to choose, and there was only a minute to decide: Was I going to tell myself this wasn't really God (when I knew that it was), or was I going to try believing it was and do something about it?

I stepped on the gas and drove around the building toward the back exit and made God a deal: "Okay, if this is you, God, then give me access to her. Maybe she's gone already. What in the world will I say to her? If you really want me to give her my shoes, then help me find her again." No sooner had I finished talking than she shuffled right in front of me.

Of course she did. You knew she was going to.

Resistance is a part of practice. There is opposition to the words of God because there is an enemy of God. The bad news is that many times the opposition will rise up from inside us even as we try to make God's words real in our life. Inside us are very powerful, well-practiced methods of resistance. We are all very good at convincing ourselves that the words of God that we think we've heard or read aren't really meant for obedience right now in real life. Resistance can also come in external forms, but anytime you actually try to do what God says, it *will* come. You should begin to expect it—awareness is a huge piece of pushing through. Resistance to God's words is a tale literally as old as time. It goes all the way back to the first man and the first woman. God spoke a word, and there was an enemy who resisted their obedience to it.

Tactics of Resistance

When God created humanity and placed Adam and Eve in a garden to live, his command to Adam was, "You must not eat from the tree of the knowledge of good and evil, for when you eat from it you will certainly die" (Gen. 2:17). It was a clear and simple order: don't eat from this one tree. It wasn't long until

Adam and Eve encountered resistance to that command. They went about their life, but one day encountered a serpent. With three small phrases to Eve, the serpent completely undermined her practice of the Word of God. The spirit of this enemy is using the same three tactics to put up resistance to the Word of God in your life as well. Eve heard the words of God loud and clear, but things got a little fuzzy when the serpent questioned what God had *really* said.

Did God really say?

Now the serpent was more crafty than any of the wild animals the LORD God had made. He said to the woman, "Did God really say, 'You must not eat from any tree in the garden'?" (Gen. 3:1)

The first phrase out of the serpent's mouth seeded doubt in the very words that God had spoken. There's a whisper that comes quickly when you try to take action on something God said, and that whisper sounds like, "You sure you got that right?" Doubt is a powerful tactic of resistance to stop you in your tracks. Expect the whisper.

The serpent repeated the command of God incorrectly, twisting it as he asked Eve this question. I can hear the kind of insinuating tone meant to confuse Eve. Perhaps she was susceptible to this resistance because she received the command secondhand from Adam. I don't know, but I do know that the serpent wanted to seed doubt, causing Eve to think twice about whether she'd heard the words from God correctly.

Resistance like this messes with your head. If you believe you misheard or misunderstood the actual words, then you'll give yourself permission to do something else. It cracks open the door to use your own judgment—to lean on your own understanding. That's exactly what the serpent was hoping for. When there is doubt and confusion about the very words you have heard, you're encountering resistance.

You will not die

"You will not certainly die," the serpent said to the woman. (v. 4)

The voice of resistance will also say, "Be reasonable! God won't really do that." The serpent told Eve in these five words that her actions didn't matter because God didn't mean what he said. If you believe your follow-through has no significance, then you have little reason to obey the words of God. The serpent was trying to reduce the consequences of disobedience. This type of resistance tells you that your actions won't really produce the outcome God's Word says. It might sound like, "Oh, calm down. It's just this one thing. God's not going to freak out."

That's pretty close to what I heard in the Target parking lot one day when I realized I forgot to pay for a lip gloss. It got stuck in a crack of my shopping cart, and I was already loading up my bags into the car when I noticed. I really wanted that lip gloss, but I really *didn't* want to take my four babies out of their car seats and go back inside to pay for it. I know what God's words say about stealing and honesty, so the resistance to it kicked in, trying to make it okay for me to ignore it this one time. Surely God would understand, right? I'm an honest person. One time wouldn't change anything in me. After all, I'm sure I've overpaid for plenty of things at Target before. They owe me. "You will not die," I heard. Not *you*. Not this *one* time. Not for *this*.

Resistance, my friends. Expect it. And take God at his Word.

For God knows

For God knows that when you eat from it your eyes will be opened, and you will be like God, knowing good and evil. (v. 5)

These three words of resistance say that God is holding out on you. The serpent wanted Eve to believe that there was good stuff that God just didn't want her to have. This voice of resistance will say you're going to miss out. The serpent suggested that following through on God's words would actually bring Eve *less* of the life she wanted. This type of resistance always tells you that there's goodness other places besides God. Eve was standing in front of a tree that looked good to her, and can't you just hear these kind of thoughts in her mind? "Come to think of it, why *wouldn't* God want me to enjoy this?" She probably imagined there was something amazing that she was being kept out of. These thoughts creep up to convince us that God's Word is meant to restrict us, that he's the killjoy in the sky. The insinuation that God is holding out on you makes you want to go after your own reward. That is exactly what Eve did. She wanted what the tree promised, and she wanted to get it apart from the Word of God. So she took it another way.

When the Spirit whispered to me, "Give her your shoes," it was this kind of resistance. It was "for God knows" because I had worked out the reward for my day, and it all hinged on these shoes. In one breath, God seemed to threaten that. My first response showed that I felt putting his words in action would make my day *worse* and I would be *less* happy. Sometimes resistance pops up in us in a split second and something in us just agrees with it. That's why you've got to be aware. See it coming. Know it will. When you hear it, you need to know there is an enemy coming against the very Word of God.

Thankfully, it's not *just* the voice of resistance you will hear in these moments; the Holy Spirit will be there, too, urging you to practice. The presence of the Spirit is what actually introduces the conflict! His job in moments like these is to take your well-developed tendency to go your own way and—if necessary—turn it into a full-blown conflict within you. The presence of the Spirit will often stoke these internal battles because his motive is to see the Word of God come to life. In you. Right now. He is there to remind you of the words you've heard and advocate for God's will over your own. Like it or not, "the Advocate, the Holy Spirit, whom the Father will send in my name, will teach you all things and will remind you of everything I have said to you" (John 14:26). When we want to go our own way, the Holy Spirit puts up a fight for you to choose the Word of God instead.

The Holy Spirit is there to remind you of what the words of Jesus sound like when you're driving to work on a random Wednesday morning. The Spirit translates the Word from Scripture and helps you understand what that looks like right in the moment. That day at the stoplight, the Holy Spirit instructed me to do something entirely consistent with the Word of God. Take your pick from any of the following verses (and many, many more). It's easy to see the theme through the Bible. And I had read every single one of them. I just wasn't thinking of them as I watched those big tube socks and flip-flops cross the street.

> Suppose a brother or a sister is without clothes and daily food. If one of you says to them, "Go in peace; keep warm and well fed," but does nothing about their physical needs, what good is it? In the same way, faith by itself, if it is not accompanied by action, is dead.
>
> James 2:15–17

> Do not withhold good from those to whom it is due,
>   when it is in your power to act.
>
> Prov. 3:27

> So do not worry, saying, "What shall we eat?" or "What shall we drink?" or "What shall we wear?" For the pagans run after all these things, and your heavenly Father knows that you need them. But seek first his kingdom and his righteousness, and all these things will be given to you as well.
>
> Matt. 6:31–33

> If anyone is poor among your fellow Israelites in any of the towns of the land the LORD your God is giving you, do not be

hardhearted or tightfisted toward them. Rather, be openhanded and freely lend them whatever they need.

Deut. 15:7–8

And I could go on. The Living Word was trying to move me toward the practice of the written Word of God. The opportunity that presented itself that day was not me making up my own Be Good Today to-do list. This was the Spirit of the Living God commanding me to practice his Word. All these words of Scripture rolled up into one simple command: *Give her your shoes.* And then there was resistance.

When you feel the battle of an internal tug-of-war, rejoice! If the Spirit wasn't at work in you and around you, you'd have no such conflict. You'd just keep your shoes and your own plans and go about your day. And you'd also never live a moment of your life within the kingdom of God. The Spirit will always advocate for you to practice the Word of God straight through resistance. He will help you in the struggle. Expect it! If you can rightly interpret what's going on inside you, it will help you see where to move. Resistance is just part of practice.

Jesus wants you out there in parking lots giving away shoes. His Spirit wants to lead you into real practice of his Word, and I certainly need to keep practicing. Let's be honest: I followed through that day, but it wasn't noble. It was definitely *practice* with a lot of room for improvement, especially the part when I threw my little fit about my pretty, new, cushioned shoes.

But Jesus is so generous with his encouragement and approval of even the simplest moments of obedience to his Word. Any act, any move, any step in his direction and he's right there saying, "Keep coming this way. You've got this." He's not the one shaking his finger at you telling you that you should have done it sooner or better. He's not the one shaming you for the other similar times you bypassed the chance to move. He's the one next to you saying, "Yaaaaasssssssss! Doesn't this feel good?! That was amazing. Let's do this again!"

I will never forget how the lady's eyes lit up when she realized I was serious. She couldn't believe I was actually giving her my shoes. I watched her walk away in them, and suddenly, my own plan for my day seemed lame in comparison to what Jesus had just let me be a part of. He gently spoke to my heart as I drove back around and parked, "Those shoes were never yours. Thanks for dropping them off for me." It's all his, friends. Sometimes you're just the one with the money, the car, and the right location for delivery.

Jesus wants you racking up hours and moments and days of hands-on practice. Most days it's simple: sacrifice the time to pray, buy someone's lunch, text that encouragement you could keep to yourself, apologize and mean it, don't roll your eyes when your boss says that thing she always says, or follow the nudge to wash the dishes that have crusted over in the staff kitchen. But then sometimes a day comes along when a word is spoken just to you for that one tiny little moment. The Word invites you into something set up just for your unique circumstances. These moments are so sweet. I want you to be aware of the resistance that's coming for you so that you don't miss the reward.

I could have kept my own reward that day. I could have had the payoff I'd arranged for myself with those shoes: a lunchtime run on a nice day and the self-satisfaction of a good workout. But instead—despite my begrudging obedience—Jesus was good enough to let me experience a much better reward that came directly from him. I didn't deserve the pleasure I felt from my Father as the woman disappeared around the corner in my shoes. It was overwhelming. It was unforgettable. I would have given away five more $100 pairs of shoes to experience just another moment of it. I got to work on my dad's business, and it felt great to make him proud.

Practice is the moment your faith gets stronger, but resistance is designed to stop that. If you can learn to see the opposition to your practice and obey anyway, you will build trust in God more quickly as you see that his words prove good and true. Believing God's words are good for your life gets a little easier over time because you witness his wisdom and his character firsthand. The rock of trust forms under your feet and your foundation is strengthened. You become a wise builder who is willing to dig down deep and push through the ground that resists you, giving the extra effort, cost, time, and fatigue, even though some onlookers may call you crazy. You just keep moving.

Tests

As you begin to stand firmly on rock, there are unique moments when God offers you a specific invitation to put his words into practice that involves a bigger cost. These moments are *tests*. In Scripture, God often tests people's commitment to the priorities and promises of his kingdom. Jesus tested men who approached him to see if they'd give up things like home, family, work, and tradition. He threatened whatever they'd been standing on as rock in their past. Whatever has provided you stability in the past—your career, relationship, family trust fund, acceptance into a particular group of people—you can expect that God will eventually test you to see if the rock you are standing on is that—or him.

He uses tests to see if you are ready for more. As you mature, he wants to give you more and see more of his promises fulfilled in your life, but you also live in a world that is constantly vying for your loyalty. Tests often come before a shift or change of what God will entrust to you.

I was sitting in my comfy chair late on New Year's Eve 2020, holding a Christmas cookie and a glass of champagne, when I saw a text on my phone. It was my cousin. Her text said, "I forgot to tell you I am starting my New Year's fast tomorrow. Want to join me? We can talk details tomorrow." I knew she began each new year with a three-week period of various kinds of fasting. But, ugh. I didn't want to. The small comforts of good food and wine were about the only pleasures left in a COVID-19 life, and I didn't want to give them up. But this text was a test, and I knew it. I had been asking God to move me into a brand-new phase of life. I was specific about what I was hoping for, and there were some ways I had thought about moving forward on my own since God was pretty quiet. However, I knew the Bible taught fasting as a significant path to spiritual breakthrough, so I interpreted her ten at night New Year's Eve text as a test from God saying something close to, "Alli, you know how I feel about this. Are you going to do this my way?"

In a test you must choose: the world or the kingdom. Tests reveal the answers to questions like: is God more important than him/her, is God better than having more money, are you really after his glory or your own, will you wait on him to come through when you could just go get it for yourself? God uses tests to display what's inside your heart on the outside of your life. The choice to believe and practice his Word at a specific, high-cost moment can be a game-changer for your life of faith.

Jesus was tested. Just before his public ministry began, God sent him into the desert. There he came face-to-face with his enemy when he had fasted for forty days (see Matt. 4). Three tests proclaimed Jesus's loyalty to the kingdom of God and to his Father above and beyond anything else. In these tests, Jesus proved his trust in his Father's ability to sustain his life, defend and protect him, and give him rewards that were worth more than any riches or kingdom of the world. When Jesus returned to begin this new phase of life, he was moving deeply in the power of the Spirit. Passing tests strengthens and prepares us for more.

Jesus taught about tests just like this in Matthew 25. He told three parables with overtones of testing. The first one was about whether virgins would remain ready and watchful for the return of the bridegroom. The second was about whether servants had invested a master's wealth for a return. The third was about whether people had cared for the sick and poor who were right in front of them. Each of them reveals a fundamental value of the kingdom that God will test us on. The questions he wants answered are: Will we remain faithful when we are tired? When it costs us something? When it looks like it won't pay off or when we don't think anyone is watching?

Tests are significant moments where we can be rewarded with more in the kingdom and he says to us, "Well done, good and faithful servant! You have been faithful with a few things; I will put you in charge of many things. Come and share your master's happiness!" (Matt. 25:21).

As the Spirit invites you to practice, there is one thing you're *not* going to do. You are not going to ask him why. At least not before you move.

I'm a "why" asker. I've annoyed more than one boss and more than one friend by asking why one too many times. I always want to know and buy into the big-picture reasoning behind things. I struggle to commit when something doesn't make sense to me, so I ask why. If you're anything like that, you're going to need to set that aside in your tests and experiments with faith. I've asked, "Why this? Why now? Why her? Why not? Why do I need to give this up?" a million times. God rarely explains all the whys up front.

When my four kids were little, we discovered they often put off being obedient to our requests with *all* the why questions! Even a simple request like, "Get your shoes on, please," would almost always be met with a "Why?!" This drove me absolutely nuts, so we implemented a rule: When you hear our words asking you to do something, **you must obey first and ask why second**. If you don't see why it was important as you obey us, then we will be happy to answer any questions you still have—but not until *after* you've actually done what we said! We found this little rule cleared up 98 percent of the why questions. Stick that one in your back pocket as you practice putting the Word of God to work in your life.

Let's move on with our practice. Push through the resistance. Pass the tests. Keep going. The heart of God in all his insistence on practice is this: he *really* doesn't want you to crash when the flood comes. I think he wept with me when my life crumbled to pieces. I think he wished I'd actually done something with his words years before that. This is why he is pressing you into and through resistance. This is why he will test you.

If you misinterpreted past resistance, you can start again. If you have let resistance discourage you in the past, you have a second chance. If you failed a test in the past, it's not too late. Today, with his Spirit, you can shatter the resistance and build something that will last. "Do not merely listen to the word, and so deceive yourselves. Do what it says" (James 1:22).

10

YOUR SIGNATURE MOVE

sat down one morning, like I always do, to read the Bible. I didn't have anything specific on my mind when I began, but I sure did as soon as I heard the words of Matthew 5. Jesus taught in these words about being reconciled with a brother or sister who "has something against you" (v. 23). The basic idea of the passage is that actually going *to reconcile* needs to take priority—even before we come to God with other things. Suddenly, all I could think of was a woman I'd known who definitely had something against me.

I closed my Bible. I knew I couldn't read another word until I somehow tried to reconcile with her. It wasn't going to do me any good to read more words in the Bible or speak more words in prayer. I'd heard the words of Jesus on this subject, and I was pretty sure he didn't want to talk anymore. He wanted me to *do* something. I spent the next twenty minutes crafting an email to a woman who disliked me more than anyone else I could think of. It had been nearly two years since our last conversation.

As you experiment with putting the words of God into action in your life, movement is the key. I had no idea what I was getting into when I invited her to meet me for coffee, but I knew it was movement in the right direction. It was most definitely an experiment. As I drove to Starbucks, I was nervous—because who wants a meeting like that? But I also felt an overriding sense of peace. I felt reassured that this meant something to God no matter what went down in the next thirty minutes. I felt more connected to him somehow. I was experiencing in real time what Jesus taught in the words of John 15. When you actually *do what his Word says*, you're connecting with God in a closer relationship.

> You are my friends if you do what I command. I no longer call you servants, because a servant does not know his master's business. Instead, I have called you friends, for everything that I learned from my Father I have made known to you. (vv. 14–15)

The way Jesus's followers were supposed to stay connected in that relationship? *Do what he commands.* In other words—move! The way we have a relationship with Jesus is to start trying to do what he says. We become friends with Jesus when we get active with his words. I know your friends don't usually say you can be friends if you do everything they say, but a relationship with Jesus works a little bit differently. The path to a relationship with him goes straight through the words of his commands because acting on, moving to, and practicing those words is where you encounter more of the Holy Spirit. The written Word of God will always lead you to the Living Word of God if you're willing to move! That's what was with me that day in the car and at Starbucks, so Jesus and I were connected. We were growing our friendship.

Jesus promised his disciples—his friends—that he would send the Spirit to help them stay connected to him and put his words into practice. The Spirit is a person—not a spiritual force. Discovering and developing a deeper connection with him through practice of the Word is the very essence of having a relationship with Jesus. That relationship won't thrive without movement and action. Christians throw around the phrase "relationship with Jesus" without really explaining it much. It's the kind of phrase that has caused more than a few eye rolls because it has become a little cliché in Christian circles—but it's probably the best way to succinctly describe what you experience *as you begin to move*. You're building a friendship with a person who is present with you as you go.

For all of us, some actions come easy and others not so much. Your life, work, quirks, past, and personality are all factors in how you practice. God has no desire to stomp out the unique image of him that you are. He likes who he made and expects you to be yourself, just like you expect from your other friends. Most of my friends have a *thing*—something they do repeatedly in our relationship with more ease, something that seems to come naturally as a part of how we relate. One friend always invites people over. One is my go-to for advice. One is always pushing me into the next adventure. One's my truth-teller who doesn't hold back. As I got to know my friends, I began to rely on them to consistently and predictably do their thing. God's goal is always that we expand our ability to move in all kinds of ways, but he also recognizes our individuality and uniqueness. Putting the Word of God into practice isn't a religious checklist of dos and don'ts. It happens through everyday moments, like Starbucks meetups, in the context of a relationship.

You have a *thing* in your friendship with Jesus. As you put his words into practice, it will emerge and become part of how you connect and communicate. You'll know to expect it, and you'll use it repeatedly over time. There is something specific that will become a telltale sign of the pattern of obedience in your life of faith. When I closed my Bible and sent that email, it was because I recognized a moment to do my thing. The invitation I sensed from the Spirit came in a way I'd learned to expect: my signature move.

What Is Your Signature Move?

Your signature move is one of three actions. These actions are at the core of experimenting with God's Word. It's how practice looks in action. It's either *obey*, *receive*, or *hustle.* These three moves come out of the lives of three men who are considered the fathers of real, living faith in the Bible: Abraham, Isaac, and Jacob. They formed the very foundation of what it looks like to have a relationship with God. The Bible calls us back over and over again to the type of faith these three men had. It wasn't perfect, but it was real. And it was a relationship. Their lives are detailed in Genesis as patriarchs of the Jewish faith (see 50:24), but they're celebrated throughout Scripture as examples of how it looks to put God's words into action in real life with a real personality and real circumstances. These three guys practiced a lot, and they also messed up a lot. They had faith that was alive and active, even being practiced at the time of their deaths. Each of them had a signature move. It was something you can see repeated in their connection with God over time. It was something that changed the trajectory of their life more than once. Your signature move will do the same—and it's one of these three things.

Obey like Abraham

The core of Abraham's faith was obedience. If this is your signature move, you are motivated by a belief that God's Word is the truth. Trust for God probably comes easier to you. Abraham believed, so obedience flowed from his trust. He was willing to go to new places and was openhanded with his stuff, even showing a willingness to pay significant cost to follow where he thought God was leading. An "I'll go where you send me" mentality was obvious in his life. If this is in your core, you may waver in your faith when the Word of God doesn't make sense to you, or when the Word you heard isn't happening yet. If you're like Abraham, your signature move is faithful obedience.

By faith Abraham, when called to go to a place he would later receive as his inheritance, obeyed and went, even though he did not know where he was going. (Heb. 11:8)

Receive like Isaac

The core of Isaac's faith was receiving a promise and standing firm on it. If you're like him, you have strength in waiting, resting. You are secure in your identity as a child of God and are confident in his favor on your life. You don't stress much about the when and how because of your confidence in God's future promises. Patience or peace may be obvious in your life. Your heart is usually in a posture of rest and trust, so you set others at ease. You probably don't struggle with anxiety much, but you might struggle with passivity—especially when sudden, decisive action is called for. If you're like Isaac, your core move of faith is to wait and receive.

By faith Isaac blessed Jacob and Esau in regard to their future. (Heb. 11:20)

Now you, brothers and sisters, like Isaac, are children of promise. (Gal. 4:28)

Hustle like Jacob

The core of Jacob's faith was hustling. He hustled in the sense of both hard work *and* manipulation. He was a man of clever moves, always striving and contending for what he was promised. If you're like Jacob, then you love a good fight for something you believe in—the more hands-on the better. You don't want to leave anything on the table that God may be willing to give you. You love the freedom to cocreate your life with God and are happy to push on boundaries. When things aren't clear, it's just a good opportunity to wrestle with God in the gray. Delays may tempt you to manipulate the outcome you think is best. You like to move first and listen to God later. If you're like Jacob, your core move of faith is the hustle it takes to contend for new ground.

> Your name will no longer be Jacob, but Israel, because you have struggled with God and with humans and have overcome. (Gen. 32:28)

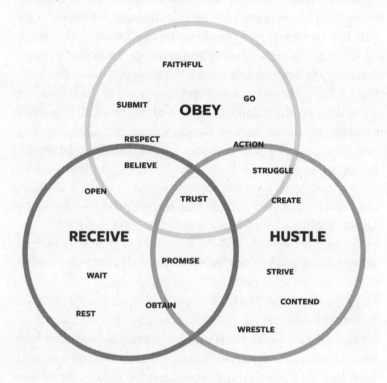

Obey, receive, or *hustle.* Over the course of their lives, all three men showed a discernable pattern. Though you can see aspects of all three moves in each story, one was most responsible for the big shifts in their lives and the legacy of faith left behind. Maturity looks like having the ability to move in all three of these ways, but the God of Abraham, Isaac, and Jacob wants to use one of these to help build your life on him.

Mine is most like Abraham: *obey.* As I've practiced my faith, I've seen obedience is my signature move. I feel an overwhelming lack of peace if I'm out of alignment with God. He knows I am motivated by a clear word, and I will obey it. If I know his Word, I get there pretty quick, so it's an easy way for us to connect. My obedience in sending the email that morning led to the next action: I found myself in my car actually driving to meet her for coffee. No one loves a potentially confrontational Starbucks date like the one I was heading to, but my obedient tendencies will drag me in, even when things seem uncertain or painful or scary. I really do trust him. I leaned on this core move again one night when I knew God was urging me to share the story of my affair with an old friend who didn't know about it. I trusted it would be good somehow on the other side, but I didn't want to talk about it. It can be exhausting. It's humbling. And, frankly, I just didn't want to. I kept feeling the Holy Spirit urge me to obey, but I kept dragging my feet. I made up excuses why I shouldn't until I finally prayed to God, "Okay, if the clock hits ten p.m. and I haven't said anything, I'm just going to blurt it out."

That's exactly what I did. I watched the digital clock go from 9:59 to 10:00, and I forced the words out of my mouth—not because I wanted to or I was feeling good about it. I did it because I didn't want to go to bed that night having disobeyed the Word I thought I was hearing. My signature move helped me practice following Jesus that night. Without it, I probably wouldn't have. Several moves of obedience have changed the course of relationships like that one—and sometimes the entire course of my life. I'm an easy get for God when it comes to obedience. Your signature move will feel the same.

The others don't come as easy for me. I tend to need a kick in the booty to insert myself into a struggle or fight for a cause, and over time I have had to practice a *lot* of waiting on God. Receiving hasn't come as naturally as just doing it myself. I've had to learn how to see and accept his favor and blessing when the thought of that makes me very uncomfortable. I've grown in all three areas, but the other two will never come quite as easily as obedience.

What do you see in your life? Naming things has power. When you can name your go-to action, you'll be amazed how many chances you see to practice. You and the Holy Spirit will have a thing, and it will become part of your relationship. Do you see a tendency toward hop-to-it obedience like Abraham? Are you at ease receiving like Isaac? Or do you find yourself always wrestling with God and others like Jacob? If you are just beginning to experiment, no worries. Start moving, and over time you will see it.

Move Like *You*

I want you to feel the freedom to practice following Jesus in a way that feels like *you* in all aspects of your life. Christians tend to have a reputation for living lives that look more like "be good" checklists rather than lives that are free to be uniquely cultivated in a relationship with their Creator. God has a life in mind for you that fits who you are. You were made to thrive in a style of connecting to God and others that's not exactly like anyone else's because of your culture, occupation, family, church, life circumstances, personality, gifts, and preferences.

In the Bible, we see normal people who connect their lives to God from wherever they live, whatever position they're in, and with whatever things they have at their fingertips. Their real life and real self was always a good enough place for God to start moving in their life: a prostitute, a boy who becomes king, a kid with a slingshot, an immigrant traveling with her mother-in-law, a poor widow, a fisherman, a Pharisee, a rich tax collector, an Ethiopian eunuch with a chariot, a Roman centurion with servants, a woman with the means to travel, a person with open guest rooms—literally every kind of normal person who was willing to use whatever they had and whoever they really were to put the words of God into practice in their life. You don't have to be someone else. You were made to practice from wherever you are now. You have a signature move, but God wants to use *every* little thing about you and *every* opportunity in your life for practicing your faith and building a life on him—like he did with a woman named Lydia (see Acts 16).

Lydia became a follower of Christ in the very earliest days of the church. She heard the gospel from Paul when he came to preach in her town called Philippi. She had a heart that was wide open, and she immediately received the truth. Her conversion was fast, and God wasted no time giving Lydia the chance to move in ways only she could. Lydia was a rich businesswoman. She had access to wealth, property, and income to support the apostles and start the church in Philippi. By the time Paul left town, she was hosting the meetings of the church in her home. Lydia was unique. She had unique resources and gifts. She also had a unique heart. She was uniquely generous. She was a leader before Paul came to town. God used all these things—and no doubt more—to create a new life for her that was built on him.

Lydia's signature move was likely *receiving*. God was able to open her heart wide to receive the gospel, and that's what catapulted her into a new life. She would have heard and believed in the future promises of God and been willing to be on the front end of those promises. She was willing to work for something at the beginning that she might never fully be able to receive. She was motivated to receive others into her home and motivated to receive others into the faith she had found. She used all her resources to do it. God took everything about Lydia and pointed it toward a new adventure because she was open and willing to receive a promise and take up her part in a new story for her life.

Every follower of Jesus has stories of starting to practice the words of Jesus—and the stories always begin exactly where they are with exactly who they are.

Ready to practice? It's time to move, and you can start right here, right now.

11

FROM RISK TO ROCK

One day at my boss's request, I walked into her office and sat down. I had given my two weeks' notice a few days before that. I was leaving my career to pursue what I thought was a God-given opportunity. My boss slid a paper across the desk and said, "Are you sure you know what you're doing?" I glanced down and saw a curved graph on the paper in front of me. Based on my current level, pay, and performance rating, it showed my projected salary and bonus structure over the coming five years. She wanted me to see in black and white what I was walking away from. I listened to her tell me about all the money that was about to come my way and promised to consider things one last time. I walked out feeling the weight of this risk and thinking, *Of* course *I don't know what I'm doing.*

I had never thought of myself as a risk-taker. Unfortunately, that self-assessment is pretty common—especially among women—but it's wrong. Risk isn't a personality trait; it's a skill you can learn, strengthen, and grow. And you must. Risk is an essential part of living out the three rhythms of *coming* to Jesus, *hearing* his Word, and putting it into *practice*. If you are trying to *come, hear,* and *practice*, then it's going to lead you straight into a risk. Warm up to it. Taking risks is critical for a strong foundation.

You've probably had more experience than you think. You need a robust view of risk if you're going to live a robust life of faith. The word *risk* conjures up images of skiing black diamond slopes but goes way beyond physical feats. It can be the willingness to start a conversation with a stranger, to try to break a long-standing habit, to give away money, or to share something vulnerable with your spouse. It might even be taking your time and energy to design a breast-pump accessory from your experience nursing five kids that you weren't sure you could get manufactured. (My brilliant friend actually did that.) Come to think of it, having five children is yet another kind of risk! You take risks all the time—the trick is to get really good at identifying the risks that *God* is putting in front of you. The risks you take on God himself are the ones that will turn your foundation to rock.

Your spiritual life will live or die based on your ability to see and take risks on God. Most of us are working with an underdeveloped view of risk, and it's keeping us on shifting ground. Wherever your foundation is weak is a place you haven't gotten good at either seeing or taking risks on God. Risk is the path on which you move toward rock. It's the way you get to the well-built life you want.

For way too long I didn't understand that following Jesus is always going to lead me to the next risk. Not expecting risks to come made them harder to face when they did—like that moment in my boss's office. "Are you sure you know what you're doing?" Her question insinuated exactly what I was afraid of; I was walking away from too much without enough information about where I was going. I wondered if the presence of risk meant the absence of God. Was my leaving this job being stupid or following Jesus?

I had internalized things about risk that weren't helpful at that moment. I remember my mom saying things like, "As a woman, don't ever put yourself in the position where you can't fully financially support yourself." I had learned to be very risk-averse with my finances. When I went to Las Vegas for the first time in my twenties, I put twenty bucks in a slot machine thinking I could entertain myself for a while on twenty-five-cent bets. I didn't understand the button that read "Bet Max," so I pushed it and my twenty bucks was gone in one pull.

I cried.

So yeah, not exactly a big gambler when it came to money. All the things I had picked up about risk over a lifetime messed with my head as I left my boss's office that day. I didn't understand a God who might just ask me to risk the very things I didn't want to.

Rhythms Lead to Risk

Like so many things in God's kingdom, the way to a strong foundation is the opposite of what you might imagine at first glance. Rock isn't formed under your life by holding tightly to things that feel safe. Rock forms for a strong, secure foundation when we walk willingly, at his invitation, into a risk to follow Jesus. I'm not talking about cliff-jumping or a Vegas roulette–type risk, but rather the ones that emerge as you live out these three rhythms of faith: *come*, *hear*, and *practice*. These three rhythms work together in a repetitive cycle that produces opportunity after opportunity to take risks on God.

Your faith in action looks like **your willingness to risk something on God**. The rhythms of come, hear, and practice work in succession to produce invitations to risk. Your faith expands a lot every time you say yes. Your foundation gets a little firmer every time you say yes. With each risk, you gather the evidence God is there, he is gracious, and he's true to his Word.

As you begin to come, hear, and practice, God loves even the tiniest risk. As with anyone else in your life, you need time and experiences with Jesus to get to know and trust him. Maybe your risk is to trust that the pattern you're seeing in your life is truly God instead of blowing it off as coincidence. Maybe you need to take a risk to simply rearrange your schedule and give God the first hour of the day to pray and read the Bible. Trust me—1 know that time is precious. My risks are often about being willing to be interrupted with my time and say yes to caring for people when it seems like my tasks won't get done. Whatever your risks are, 1 promise you this: God is going to prove himself faithful. Give him the chance to show you. He is good enough to show patience with your doubt and do something huge in your life with the smallest speck of real faith, as Jesus said in Matthew 17:20: "Truly I tell you, if you have faith as small as a mustard seed, you can say to this mountain, 'Move from here to there,' and it will move. Nothing will be impossible for you."

Risk Builds Relationships

The whole point is to grow your relationship with God, so risk begets risk. Think of it as a snowball effect. Once you find him faithful and good, your willingness to trust grows, and faith begins to snowball in your life. As you risk, your willingness to risk grows, and your relationship becomes more solid. As 1 get to know a friend, 1 naturally entrust more and more of my confidence in them. It's the same with God. We all start off not knowing him very well! It's fair to need some basic stuff answered. I need to build confidence in the answers to questions like, Are you really there, God? Do you really like me? Are you good? Will you show up for me? You wouldn't immediately know these things about a person, and God doesn't expect you to skip over this phase with him, either. The best relationships keep expanding and keep proving to you over and over again that the answer to those questions is yes. Give yourself the grace to go through the same relationship-building process with God. He has patience and grace for you to start wherever you really are—no need to pretend you trust him if you don't.

I have a friend who said she thought back to the first risk she ever took on God, and it was simply talking to him. Out loud. Like he was actually there. That's a great start! Based on her experience and her past, it was a risk to believe there was even a God who could hear her when she spoke to him. Bingo! That's a real risk on God. That's an act of faith.

I had one of these decision points with God in an elevator. I had already asked God to help me get out of the affair I was in at work. It was ruining my life. It was eating away at me from the inside, and I wanted to be free. I didn't know how to get out without causing even more devastation. As I rode up the elevator at work one day, I realized God was giving me an invitation to take a risk on him. I was thinking of the words I'd read in the Bible: "If you hold to my teaching, you are really my disciples. Then you will know the truth, and the truth will set you free" (John 8:31–32).

I realized Jesus was showing me how to break free. We are set free not by knowing the truth but by *doing* the truth. I can't even fully know the truth until I am brave enough to hold to the teachings of Jesus! As I turned the words over in my mind, suddenly I knew the risk God wanted me to take. I was going to have to open my mouth and speak the words. I needed to willingly confess.

This was a huge risk. I knew I might lose the marriage I was trying to hold on to. But I couldn't deny in that one silent moment in the elevator God was urging me to believe his Word by doing it. All the things I knew about repentance, heart change, and forgiveness were coming into view. Did I really believe that God's way through it would actually lead me to life? I committed to him in the quiet of my heart on a sixty-second elevator ride. "Okay, God," I said, "whatever happens, whatever it means for my life, I am just going to tell the truth. No matter what it costs me. I want to be free." I was pretty sure this risk was going to be the death of everything I held dear. And I felt I deserved whatever pain was coming my way. I was terrified.

That night I went home and confessed. Everything got much worse. All I felt was guilt and pain and despair—not just that day but for months and months to come. I cried myself to sleep repeatedly. I lived in shame for a long time. Needless to say, the risk did not seem to pay off. But now, many years removed, I know for certain that, in the end, it was this risk that saved our marriage. The risk that God invited me to take on him that day in the elevator was what allowed us to begin to eventually rebuild. We would both look back and say that it was that proactive confession that was the first glimmer of the possibility of trust and integrity. Jesus already knew that, but I had to follow through to find out if he was right, if his Word was good. I could have ignored the invitation to tell the truth. I could have tried to bury this awful thing. But not if I wanted to be standing on Jesus in my marriage. To stand on him, I had to risk.

He turned out to be so very right and so very faithful. Yes, it was slow. Yes, there were a lot of moments I wondered if we were going to make it. In the end, though, it was only the truth that could ever have been strong enough to build on again. Some risks are tiny. Some are huge. Jesus loves any size risk you take because it's the faith he wants to see. He is inviting you to come and see that anytime you stand on him, you end up standing in the end.

Say yes.

Whatever it is, do it.

Risk Forms Rock

Watch him show up for you, and when he does, the ground under your feet will turn to rock. Trusting in him is better than clinging to a job. He is a stronger rock than the relationship you're terrified to lose. He will bring you more peace than the money you think you need. His smile will lift you up far more than the approval of the one person you so desperately want it from. Rock won't happen by holding on tight to what looks secure right now. Counterintuitively, rock only happens through risk.

The first risk is always the hardest. Learning to trust God happens little by little. Be gentle with yourself. It isn't easy. You don't have to think of yourself as a risk-taker to become one; you just have to want to follow Jesus. Every real follower of Jesus—starting with the very first follower—has always had to take risks:

> As Jesus was walking beside the Sea of Galilee, he saw two broth-ers, Simon called Peter and his brother Andrew. They were casting a net into the lake, for they were fishermen. "Come, follow me," Jesus said, "and I will send you out to fish for people." At once they left their nets and followed him. (Matt. 4:18–20)

The day I left my nets to follow him was awfully scary. It wasn't just leaving the security of my salary, but the entire plan I'd had for my life. The numbers just made it real. I was taking a big-time professional and financial risk in giving up a career the same way Peter and Andrew did. The way I managed it was the same way they did—only by the grace of God and through countless battles with doubt. It'll be the same for you, too, no matter what size risk. Waiting for beyond-a-shadow-of-a-doubt certainty takes things out of the realm of faith.

"Come, follow me" was Jesus's invitation to take a risk. Not all of us are going to leave careers to follow Jesus, but we will all walk away from significant expectations for our own life in order to take up a life following Christ instead—and these risks or opportunities often come when you least expect it. Noah had never seen rain when God invited him to build a boat. Abraham agreed to pack up and move when he didn't even know the destination. Ruth went to a country where she knew her chances of finding a husband were somewhere near zero. Abigail knew there were hundreds of armed men on the way to kill her husband, and she went out alone to stop them. Mary was an unmarried teenager who had to tell her fiancé that God got her pregnant. You can add your name to the list of people who found that God had gone before them, who learned that God was true to his Word, and who were standing in the end.

Doubt is going to come hand in hand with risk. In no way does it negate the faith—it's part of it! When I was in my boss's office that day, her question "Are you sure you know what you're doing?" was like a whisper in my ear telling me the lie that if I had *any* doubt, then it couldn't be right, that it couldn't be God. Don't sweat your doubt. It isn't the outcome you need to be sure of; it's *your God* that you need to be sure of. Risk—by definition—cannot happen outside of uncertainty. Faith happens when there's something you can't quite fully see. So your confidence has to be *in God*; not in the outcome. "Now faith is confidence in what we hope for and assurance about what we do not see" (Heb. 11:1).

Faith doesn't grow because you get what you want but because you get to know God in the process of trust. What is the risk God is putting in front of you? If you say yes, you're going to have an experience that will teach you something about who God is and what he's like. Next time, you'll trust him more. Faith grows through taking risks on the person, power, provision, plans, and perfections of God—not because it all goes smoothly and turns out well.

Faith doesn't grow because you get a good outcome. My husband could tell you that. After he took a risk to go on a mission trip and spent time, money, and vacation days, it was a total disaster. He got terribly ill, couldn't work for three full days of the trip, and inexplicably lost his vision in a foreign country with no health care available and a young son along. But today he would say it was worth it. Not because it was any less of a disaster but because he discovered parts of God in Nicaragua that he'd never seen or known before. Faith grows when you find out you can stand on the rock. We are all unsure of this mysterious, invisible, risky God. None of us have seen him with our own eyes, but I know he's got you. There's so much grace for you to risk getting to know him.

> Though you have not seen him, you love him; and even though you do not see him now, you believe in him and are filled with an inexpressible and glorious joy, for you are receiving the end result of your faith, the salvation of your souls. (1 Pet. 1:8–9)

Risk On Repeat

There is no limit to the number of times you can go around the circle. These three rhythms can repeat endlessly for a lifetime, producing untold numbers of risks to grow your faith. Faith is not a static concept: it's a dynamic, changing phenomenon with incredible potential for growth. Even the disciples who spent a couple years directly in the presence of Jesus had to keep growing in their faith. Jesus had to still command them to believe even *after* they'd seen and believed that he was the Christ. There is always more to believe. Faith isn't meant to stay the same size and in the same place as the first moment you believe.

As you *come* and *hear* and *practice*, God will never stop uncovering new opportunities to trust him in places you aren't standing on rock yet. I love the words from the man who wanted Jesus to perform a healing: "I do believe; help me overcome my unbelief!"

(Mark 9:24). I've turned that into my own prayer many times. *Jesus, I believe! Help me trust you in the places inside me that still don't want to risk believing you.*

Too many Christians believe God's objective is to help them find a safe and comfortable life when *risk* is actually his MO. If we don't expect it as part of our spiritual life, then risk may feel off or bad or wrong when it is truly the key to thriving. The day you put something real on the line is the day you start digging for rock. Firmer and firmer faith is won only by moving into experimentation through what you uncover as you rhythmically come to him, hear his Word, and practice it daily, over and over again. A foundation on the rock isn't formed in one round of come, hear, practice. It is formed slowly but surely over many repetitions through these cycles and saying yes to as many risks as possible.

All of us need personal experiences with God that provide unique, deep, convincing evidence that Jesus is able to be the foundation of our entire lives. I have a friend who's had to risk by depending on God for her next meal, her kids' clothes, and her house payment. She experienced needing an extra $250 for her house payment and going to the mailbox to find a rebate check in that exact amount. She prayed for a way to afford winter clothes for her kid and opened the front door to a bag of sweaters in the size she needed from a friend who had cleaned out her closet. She knows God in highly personal ways in the exact spots she was prone to freaking out and feeling insecure. God knows the places of unbelief in you, and he's going to offer you a risk to take that will prove he is enough in that very spot.

Risk Produces Real Followers

Sometimes it feels like God targets the very things you hold on to the tightest. Because he does! Through Scripture, it's clear to see that God challenges his people whenever they rely on something besides him for their security. The risks God will ask you to take often feel like they hit you where it hurts, right in the places you most hope he won't ask you to risk anything. I believe he has set a risk in front of you right now. Whatever you hold tightest to in order to feel safe and secure might be the very place he begins to make you a real follower. Jesus wants you to be more than a believer in your mind. He wants you to be a *follower* because only followers get to have a foundation of rock.

Avoiding risks on God will always lead to building on sand. Remember the builder who built on the hard, sandy ground in the parable of the wise and foolish builders? He didn't want to risk the time or energy or discomfort of digging down to the rock. He went with (what looked like) the low-risk building scenario, the hard summertime ground for easier, faster building. But in the rainy season, that ground turned out to be a huge mistake.

Jesus wants you to risk following him *now*, before the rainy season. When you don't see or take the risks that God lays in front of you, you always ensure instability later. Proactive risk to move in his direction always turns out better in the end.

> I warned you when you felt secure,
> but you said, "I will not listen!"
> This has been your way from your youth;
> you have not obeyed me.
>
> (Jer. 22:21)

I tend to push hard when it comes to this subject because I really believe this keeps so many believers from becoming deeply grounded followers of Christ. I think it's time to stop talking yourself into being more reasonable at the very moment you have the opportunity to actually experience a living God! Believe me, I know how hard it is to trust him. I know how terrifying it is to wonder if he'll really come through for you. But I'm willing to be the one to give you a shove if I have to! Just like I did with my son when we were zip-lining.

We were at Family Camp, and he was five. He was a fun, physical kid, so I figured he'd love zip-lining. I signed us up, and we climbed the platform to the dual zip lines when it was our turn. It was then I realized I'd made a significant miscalculation about how he'd feel.

He. Freaked. Out.

He wouldn't let them clip him to the line. He cried and moaned; he looked at me with terrified eyes, begging me not to make him do it. I pulled out *all* my best parenting moves, my sweetest voice of patience and encouragement, and my most convincing tales of the glory awaiting him. None of it worked. I even let the girls behind us go so he could watch them jump and see how much fun they had. Finally, I was done. I looked at the guy working the lines and said, "Put him on." I held him tightly while he was crying and kicking me while the guy clipped him on the line. I got clipped to mine. The worker thought I was insane, but I knew my child. I knew him to his core. I knew he would love it. I knew he'd hate himself if we climbed down the steps and went back to his daddy. I just *knew* he needed to do this. (And no, I don't recommend this to you as a normal parenting tactic.) I said to the guy, "On the count of three, I want you to push him off. One, two, three!" I made the worker shove my screaming kid off the platform.

And five seconds later, he was squealing in delight. He yelled over to me while we were sailing along together, "This is amaaaaaz-ing! Wheeeeee! And don't tell Daddy I cried!"

We are so like this when it comes to trusting God. I want you to jump off the platform when God invites you to risk with him. I'd push you if I could because the jump is scary, but there's free-dom on the other side. Our question is always "What if it goes wrong?" But I want you to start asking yourself the question my favorite poem by Erin Hanson poses instead: "What if you fly?"

Do it! Follow him! He's never going to let you down.

What is the risk God wants you to take?

I can already see the rock just waiting to form under your feet.

12

REBUILT ON THE ROCK

Not many of us get very far into life without waking up one day and realizing we've somehow become the foolish builder:

> But the one who hears my words and does not put them into practice is like a man who built a house on the ground without a foundation. The moment the torrent struck that house, it collapsed and its destruction was complete. (Luke 6:49)

Everything is fine, and then the land under your feet just gives way—sometimes without warning or explanation. The relationship that was for keeps walked out on you. You promised yourself never again and did it one too many times. You've chased the wrong things because of motivations in your own heart you didn't fully understand. You knew exactly what God would want and chose the opposite. I've missed the ground shifting under my feet too. Pieces of my life and my relationships have collapsed too. Sometimes the fall is the only sign you can't ignore that you weren't standing on rock.

The shocking grace from God about any collapse is this: the fall is already part of your rebuilding. God is at work in the flood.

His grace on your life cannot be stopped by rising waters, unstable parts of your life, or even by something falling completely apart. God's grace can and will reach you anywhere. The very things that have broken into rubble can be the beginning of rock forming under your feet again. If you are at the bottom, God can rebuild you. When you bottom out, he is already in the process of doing it. The Holy Spirit is no less present with you and is just as capable to rebuild the pieces of your life that didn't hold up.

Now, I admit, when you're looking at pieces that have crumbled around you, this parable doesn't feel like comfort. It feels like an "I told you so." But Jesus's words in the parable of the wise and foolish builders can be read from two perspectives, both in the here and now and for all eternity. There is a day coming when Jesus will return, and the present era will pass away. In that day, if you aren't standing on the rock, there is no rebuilding what's been lost. The destruction described here will be final—*complete*. But that day is not today! Today you have *right here* and *right now*. You still have the chance to get up. You still have the chance to rebuild any part of your life to stand on the rock. Don't sweep up a pile of rubble and try to stand on it. Lay a foundation of solid rock while you have the chance. You can do it even from a collapse if you will *come* to him. *Hear* his Word. Put it into *practice.*

The same rhythms in your life that build also rebuild what's fallen down. God can make anything stay standing. I've lived the truth of that, but there is no rebuilding without taking a good look at where you are right now. You could very well be in a sinkhole.

Sinkholes Happen

When you're down there, it's hard to face what can be a long, slow process of standing up again. And the truth is—most often—rebuilding anything that will last *is* long and slow. Your instincts and experience tell you that, which is why sinkholes feel so overwhelming. I know what it feels like to open your eyes in the morning and feel the weight of your own mistakes crashing down on you all over again. I know the bliss of the split second between sleep and wake before you remember that you have to climb out of the bad reputation you made for yourself. I know what it's like to face a part of your life where the ladder leading out of the hole seems so high that you can't bring yourself to step on even one rung. I get how overwhelming it is to believe something that looks dead could have a new life. It feels like the words of Psalm 69:

> Rescue me from the mire,
> do not let me sink;
> deliver me from those who hate me,
> from the deep waters.
> Do not let the floodwaters engulf me
> or the depths swallow me up
> or the pit close its mouth over me.
>
> (vv. 14–15)

That's a sinkhole prayer.

In Israel there actually are sinkholes. They've formed in a region around the Dead Sea.

I got to go there when I visited Israel, but it wasn't at all what I expected. Just about everything going on in the land and water of the region has to do with *salt*. The first surprise was the little lecture we got before leaving the van about not messing around near the water. Not only does the salt make the shoreline rubbery and slippery but if you fall face-first and swallow a bunch of water, it might just kill you. This is not normal beachy saltwater; it's over ten times that. The salt means nothing lives there. No form of life is possible in the water or land nearby—no fish, no insects, no birds, no vegetation. Nothing. I left the van wide-eyed and inched away from the two goofballs in our group.

When you swim in the sea, the salt makes for a crazy, amazing experience. You can sit up in the water like you're sitting in a chair! The water literally holds you up because the salt creates such high buoyancy levels. But it's a different story when all that salt ends up in the land. Salt isn't rock. Salt doesn't hold things up very well.

Minerals will always drain to the lowest elevation, and the Dead Sea is the lowest point of elevation on the earth, so it is full of minerals like salt that have drained out of rock and flowed there in mass quantities over time. The sinkholes are unique to this region of Israel because of the extremely high salt content of the land. As the water level of the Dead Sea has dropped, all that salt gets left behind in the surrounding land. This is actually what's creating sinkholes. Salt dissolves when fresh water comes.

Remember those rain patterns in Israel? Well, they still happen today—not just when Jesus was giving the Sermon on the Mount. The freshwater Jordan still runs right into the Dead Sea region, and it still floods. As the fresh water from the Jordan soaks into the salt-filled earth, the salt is dissolved! This creates pockets of air below the surface of the ground where the salt used to be. As the Jordan repeatedly floods the area over time like it always has, these pockets of air have gotten bigger and bigger—until they just can't hold anything up anymore. Eventually the ground gives way. A sinkhole happens. Sinkholes in Israel and in our own lives happen because there's not enough rock. The salt just isn't strong enough to hold anything up. Only rock does that.

Some parts of our lives are being held up by salt. It's true for all of us. The foundations we think are strong are really fragments of worldly wisdom, things that worked in the past, pieces of our parents' advice, scar tissue—a lot of salt that's flowed downhill and piled up in the lowest places inside us. It's not strong. It's just what we've learned to stand on. Salt deposits hold things up for a while, but they're really fragile. When we try to build something solid into our lives and find some of this salty stuff from our past, we discover the rock under us isn't steady. Our foundation is full of salt. Without enough rock, when a flood hits our life—sinkhole! The collapse looks sudden, but it isn't; the salt's been collecting there for a long time.

There are researchers who monitor the Dead Sea region for changes in the ground, trying to predict the timing of the collapse. It's difficult because any sequence of images from the observations could show nothing, nothing, nothing, and then a sudden collapse.

> But the one who hears my words and does not put them into practice is like a man who built a house on the ground without a foundation. The moment the torrent struck that house, it collapsed and its destruction was complete. (Luke 6:49)

A sinkhole in our own lives *looks* like a similar story of nothing, nothing, nothing, and then a sudden collapse, but it really isn't. It's a story that happens in our lives slowly over time as the fresh water soaks in. Most collapses in our own lives are the same, caused by something going on below the surface for much, much longer.

But the good news is that it's a freshwater flood that created the sinkhole! I know that doesn't sound like good news, but it is.

The Jordan River is what's creating the sinkholes in Israel because its fresh, pure water is coming in and dissolving the impurities. This might not be good news for the actual land region, but it is good news for us. When something in our lives collapses, God is already at work! He has been slowly flooding our lives. He isn't interested in us being held up by salt. He wants to dissolve anything that isn't going to help us stay standing. Sometimes there's enough salt in some part of our lives that when the flood comes in, we find ourselves at the bottom of a sinkhole.

But take heart if you're at that point in your life right now. *The flood and the sinkhole are part of your rebuilding.* Jesus is already on the move in your life, getting rid of any part of your foundation that isn't rock. Jesus will flood your life with his fresh, living water to dissolve the salt. He's doing it on purpose—not to be mean, but so that you can build on the rock. It has to go. That relationship, that career, those kids, that money—they were never going to hold you up anyway. If you're in a sinkhole with one of them in pieces, there is a tiny part of you that can breathe a sigh of relief because God is at work. He won't settle for less in your lives. He wants you to build on only rock.

As I look back over the last twenty years or so, I can see the floodwaters that rose in my life were not something separate from the work of God. They were used by God to produce change. Yes, my own sin, mistakes, and shortcomings created floods and rising water, as they often do, but they also dissolved things that needed to go. I have watched pride, unforgiveness, scarcity, fear, self-hatred, isolation, lies, bad communication patterns, people-pleasing, and all other kinds of salt in my foundation get dissolved by having to deal with troubles—and sometimes collapses—in my life. And now there is rock in many of those places. The strength that replaced it makes it impossible to look back and wish for anything different, even though the flood is never fun.

Floods damage. I hate the damage, but the floods are simultaneously the living water of Jesus—the Holy Spirit—flowing into and around your life. Jesus wants you to rebuild whatever has fallen on him. Only him. The storms I thought were going to take me under were exactly what brought me to Jesus. This is the reason I can't hate my past—because now I can't look back and see anything but his work through my storms. Anything I rebuilt out of that place is still standing in my life today. This was the time I stumbled into these rhythms. I reached out for God at the bottom of a sinkhole. I came. I heard. I practiced. I had no idea that was going to rebuild my life, but it did.

Come, Hear, Practice—Even from the Sinkhole

As I sought God in the aftermath of my affair, I took some time off work. Every morning I would wake up and spend time alone with God, mostly because I didn't have anyone else. I'd talk to him or cry with him. I prayed a lot and asked him to be there with me because I felt so alone. I didn't have anywhere else to be, so day after day, for several weeks in a row, I just kept coming back. I wasn't sure if he heard me at all, but as I slowly came to him day after day, I began to sense that even in—or maybe especially because of—my broken heart and the mess of my life, he really was there. There was no reason for me not to be honest, so I was.

Day after day, I started to experience the truth of what Psalm 34:18 says: "The LORD is close to the brokenhearted and saves those who are crushed in spirit." I started asking God all my questions about my future—like should I stay in this job or leave, or is there anyone who could be my friend right now, or am I going to end up divorced, or can you help me understand why I ever did this? I remember being in my kitchen listening to a worship song, and I started to sing to him from my heart. I will never forget this moment because I experienced the palpable presence of the Spirit for the very first time. He filled the room, and I knew he was there. But I couldn't make any sense of it! I felt entirely at fault for the storms and floods I was in. Why was he around me when I was the worst person I knew? Yet in those same rising waters had come the very presence of God. Right into my kitchen.

During the time I spent with him each day I'd read the Bible I got familiar with his Word again. I read about all kinds of people who had screwed up. For some reason, I'd had the impression that the Bible was filled with judgment, rules, and saints, but instead I found liars, adulterers, and sinners like me in its pages. This didn't make sense to me either, but I sure was relieved. I also read the book of Romans and heard the Word loud and clear that said without Jesus, I am a slave to sin. I had sure lived that truth, and it was ugly. But with him, "there is now no condemnation for those who are in Christ Jesus" (8:1). These words made so much sense of the motivations and desires inside me that led me astray and seemed stronger than the good in me. But I learned that the presence of the Spirit changes everything. And—wow—did I need to hear those words of freedom, power, and new life. I also found out in the words of Psalm 139 that there is a God who made me and knew everything about me and what I was going through and planned to stay with me in the depths and lead me in his ways.

What a relief to know I wasn't finished. What a relief to find out there was a way to stand up again.

Occasionally during this time, I would get an idea about something I needed to do. Sometimes it was an apology I needed to make, a conversation I needed to have, a boundary I needed to set, something in my house I needed to get rid of, a conversation to have with my husband, or a certain question to ask my counselor. As I got these thoughts, I would just do them. I was in a position where I really had nothing to lose. I wasn't protecting myself. I wasn't protecting anything in my life because I was pretty sure it was all completely destroyed anyway. I accidentally stumbled into the secret of being a true disciple of Jesus:

> Trust in the LORD with all your heart
> and lean not on your own understanding;

in all your ways submit to him,
    and he will make your paths straight.
                (Prov. 3:5–6)

Again, the flood had brought me to the feet of Jesus, and I was finally willing to get up and follow. I don't think he cared one bit that I did it because I had nothing else to lose. In this season, Jesus got down on his hands and knees underneath me. He let me stand on him when I didn't think I could stay upright. For the first time, he became my rock. I knew I couldn't go forward without him. And it all started with the flood.

Come, hear, and practice are not just the rhythms of faith when all is well and you can proactively dig for the rock of a strong foundation; they're also the ones that will help you stand up again when you collapse. The work of God is coming in the same fresh water as your flood. If you're in a collapse right now of any kind, your storm has also brought living water. It might dissolve all your salt, but the salt was never going to hold you up. You were always headed for the collapse—getting there in the here and now is the kindness and the mercy of God for you. You don't want to live your whole life and find out later it wasn't really sitting on the rock.

It's not too late to rebuild. As a matter of fact, the flood means you're already in the process! Don't stay on the bottom of your sinkhole in fear or shame or regret. I know what it's like to not want to go home. I know what it feels like to look in the mirror and confront the person you *are* instead of the one you thought you were *going* to be. I've been the foolish builder who only considered what God had to say after I made sure I was going to get what I wanted. I've loved money, approval, and success more than God sometimes. I've had plenty of salt in my foundation just like you do in yours. But come to Jesus. Hear his Word. Follow him. He has so much more for you than a pile of salt.

Stand Up Again

The Jordan River is everywhere in the Bible. It is often used as a symbol from God to cross over and move to something new—to receiving a promise. In the Old Testament, when it was time for Israel to receive the land God promised his people, they needed to carefully follow his presence since they'd never been that way before (see Josh. 3:4). He led them straight to the edge of the Jordan River—*at flood stage.* God instructed them to walk right into the rising waters. It wasn't until they were standing in the flood that he took them miraculously to the other side. God was never going to abandon them there. He wanted their trust. He wanted them to come to him even in the flood. He wanted them to hear his Word. He wanted them to follow his way out.

He wants that for you too. Sometimes the flood is part of your rebuilding. I want to say I'm sorry if that's the case for you (and I am sorry for the pain!), but I am not sorry for what God will do in your life as a result. He is the ultimate foundation, the ultimate builder, the unbreakable rock. Keep coming to him. Keep hearing his Word. Keep practicing it every day. You're going to get through the rising waters. You're going to survive the collapse.

Israel struggled with God in the same way we do; it was a story of ups and downs. Even after they crossed the Jordan and God tried to rebuild them for the future, they eventually collapsed again. Big time. This time it looked like God just stood by and watched, even staying silent. (And you thought you were the only one who ever thought that about God.) It looked like their collapse was final. Complete. Over. Their nations were destroyed. But way back before their fall, God had already promised to rebuild them.

The prophet Jeremiah said, "I will bring Judah and Israel back from captivity **and will rebuild them** as they were before" (Jer. 33:7, emphasis mine). God was in the flood, the trouble, the storms, the enemies, the rising waters. Yes, it came about because of their sin and disobedience to God, and he was also in those things, dissolving their false foundations, pushing them toward the promised rebuilding.

You have never once been forgotten by God in your flood or in your sinkhole. You have that same promise of rebuilding in Christ. When the bottom of my life fell out, I knew I deserved to be left—by both my husband and God. But I also felt his compassion for me. I experienced his presence, power, and promises to me during the worst of it. Against all odds, in a move of radical grace, neither of them left me. I was forgiven, and my life was able to be rebuilt into something stronger than what it ever could have been before because now I was standing on the rock. A bunch of my salt was dissolved in one huge flood, and that same flood was the grace of God to me in Christ. I started to believe I could actually be rebuilt into someone new.

Rebuilding is possible because of the foundational work of Jesus on the cross. Romans 5:8 says, "But God demonstrates his own love for us in this: While we were still sinners, Christ died for us." Right at the moment, when I least deserved it, he came to me to rebuild my life. He did the same for you. As you begin to come, hear, and practice following him, Romans 6:4 says you can be "buried with him through baptism into death in order that, just as Christ was raised from the dead through the glory of the Father, we too may live a new life."

You get to live a new life on the foundation of the cross. You do *not* get what you deserve. You get grace instead. Grace is terribly, beautifully unfair, and it's yours for the taking. Not everyone in your life will be happy about your rebuilding, but when God promises a rebuild, he does it. Look past the haters and keep coming, hearing, and practicing, and the strength you build will make itself known in time.

One woman came to me after I'd served in my local church faithfully for nearly twenty years and said that she worked on the same floor of my company many years back when I had the affair. She had always doubted me when I went into ministry. She doubted my integrity, my character, my honesty, my marriage, my children, my qualification for ministry—basically everything about my life. She admitted she'd slandered me to anyone who would listen to her. She hated the fact that my life had been redeemed. To her great credit, she confessed all this to me because she wanted to ask for my forgiveness and apologize. I forgave her. Not one bit of what she'd done impacted my rebuilding. God laid me a foundation in Christ that nothing on earth could crumble. He promised to rebuild my foundation and he did it. I believe the words of Philippians 1:6 for you too: "He who began a good work in you will carry it on to completion until the day of Christ Jesus." I believe in God's ability to recreate you and any part of your life. The foundation for a new life is always possible when Jesus is involved. When the Spirit draws you, come to him with your heart and believe he will do it. What God starts, God finishes.

Whenever I get a glimpse of a life being rebuilt, I just agree with Jesus that it's possible—even if it looks like destruction from a flood at first. If he's there, it's going to happen. Rising waters and the sinkholes often come before the strongest foundations. He's enough to hold you up while you come, hear, and practice your way to standing again.

> Therefore, if anyone is in Christ, the new creation has come: The old has gone, the new is here! (2 Cor. 5:17)

Come to him.
Hear his Word.
Practice it with your life.
If you do, your feet will get all the way down to the Rock. And this time, you're going to stay standing.

ACKNOWLEDGMENTS

This book wouldn't have been possible without the following people:

Jesus who opened the doors and went ahead of me in the most astounding ways. This is truly a book made possible by his Spirit at work. At the beginning of this long process, I was asked who I knew that could help me make connections to bring this to life. I answered, "I only know Jesus." If you only know one person, that's the right one.

My kids Andrew, Hope, Luke, and Zoe who each encouraged me and believed in me alongside their dad, Bill, to whom this book is dedicated. I look forward to seeing all the beautiful stories that God will unfold in our lives. I pray that mine will become part of your strong foundations. Stand on him.

My friend Krissy who frustratingly insisted that I don't make any sense without the full story.

And the other incredible women God has used for wisdom, counsel, help, strengthening, encouragement, and comfort as this book was written: Amanda, Elizabeth, Kirstin, Trisha, Andrea, Lisa, Bronwyn, Amy, Laura, and Beth. Each of you met me in a tiny moment that ended up being huge.

Thank you.

DIG DOWN TO THE ROCK

A Guide to Deeper Reflection and Study

CHAPTER 1

Fill in the blanks from these lines in chapter 1:
If you are with a group, discuss which is most relevant to you.

- Even though _____ is inevitable, _____ is not.

- _____ rarely see the crash coming.

- . . . to build without putting in the extra care or effort to find _____ for a foundation would have been so much easier.

- A faith built through the continual rhythms of _____, _____, and _____ will put you on the rock and will build you what lasts.

Use your favorite translation to write out Proverbs 10:25.

Which one of these best describes where you are right now?
If you are with a group, share and explain.

- I'm experiencing a collapse or crash; something I built is in pieces.
- I'm recovering or rebuilding from a crash or collapse.
- I feel or sense unsteadiness; the ground is shifting under my life somehow right now.
- Everything in my life seems solid, so I'm not really thinking about any cracks.
- I'm looking to proactively strengthen my life and have Jesus as more of my foundation.

What are you building in your life right now?
If you are with a group, share and explain.

- Describe any way God is involved, if at all.
- Who or what is the foundation of it?
- If you are successful, who will benefit from it?

Read Genesis 11:1–9.

Now the whole world had one language and a common speech. As people moved eastward, they found a plain in Shinar and settled there.

They said to each other, "Come, let's make bricks and bake them thoroughly." They used brick instead of stone, and tar for mortar. Then they said, "Come, let us build ourselves a city, with a tower that reaches to the heavens, so that we may make a name for ourselves; otherwise we will be scattered over the face of the whole earth."

But the Lord came down to see the city and the tower the people were building. The Lord said, "If as one people speaking the same language they have begun to do this, then nothing they plan to do will be impossible for them. Come, let us go down and confuse their language so they will not understand each other."

So the Lord scattered them from there over all the earth, and they stopped building the city. That is why it was called Babel—because there the Lord confused the language of the whole world. From there the Lord scattered them over the face of the whole earth.

Why do you think God would purposely frustrate their effort to build?

If you are with a group, discuss.

Now read Genesis 12:1–3.

The Lord had said to Abram, "Go from your country, your people and your father's household to the land I will show you.

> "I will make you into a great nation,
>   and I will bless you;
> I will make your name great,
>   and you will be a blessing.

I will bless those who bless you,
    and whoever curses you I will curse;
and all peoples on earth
    will be blessed through you."

Find the part of each of the two passages from Genesis above where a name is being made great and compare/contrast.

Read both versions of the parable of the wise and foolish builders in the Gospels.
Take time to note at least ten observations of what this parable is saying. *If you are with a group, share all your observations and decide on the most important three.*

As for everyone who comes to me and hears my words and puts them into practice, I will show you what they are like. They are like a man building a house, who dug down deep and laid the foundation on rock. When a flood came, the torrent struck that house but could not shake it, because it was well built. But the one who hears my words and does not put them into practice is like a man who built a house on the ground without a foundation. The moment the torrent struck that house, it collapsed and its destruction was complete. (Luke 6:47–49)

Therefore everyone who hears these words of mine and puts them into practice is like a wise man who built his house on the rock. The rain came down, the streams rose, and the winds blew and beat against that house; yet it did not fall, because it had its foundation on the rock. But everyone who hears these words of mine and does not put them into practice is like a foolish man who built his house on sand. The rain came down, the streams rose, and the winds blew and beat against that house, and it fell with a great crash. (Matt. 7:24–27)

What do you notice about this parable?

1.

2.

3.

4.

5.

6.

7.

8.

9.

10.

What kind of storm comes regularly in your life?
If you are with a group, share and explain.

Read 1 Corinthians 3:10–15:

By the grace God has given me, I laid a foundation as a wise builder, and someone else is building on it. But each one should build with care. For no one can lay any foundation other than the one already laid, which is Jesus Christ. If anyone builds on this foundation using gold, silver, costly stones, wood, hay or straw, their work will be shown for what it is, because the Day will bring it to light. It will be revealed with fire, and the fire will test the quality of each person's work. If what has been built survives, the builder will receive a reward. If it is burned up, the builder will suffer loss but yet will be saved—even though only as one escaping through the flames.

If you are with a group, discuss the following questions:

- **What does this passage have in common with the words of Jesus in this parable?**
- **Who or what is the foundation?**
- **What enables a foundation to be laid?** (*Hint: it's the first handful of words!*)
- **What happens to everything we build?**

COME: Fill in the blanks from these lines in the introduction to the practice of "Come."

To come is to bring the fullness of yourself—not just your _____, but your _____ and _____ and _____ as well.

Coming is _____. It's between you and him. It's entirely about the position of your _____ and your willingness to dig deep for an authentic exchange with a _____ God.

How would you describe the attitude and position of your heart toward God right now?
If you are with a group, discuss why this is the case.

Is there a time you have actually come to Jesus? If so, when, why, where, and with whom?
If you are with a group, share and discuss any commonalities you find in these instances.

CHAPTER 2

Fill in the blanks from these lines in chapter 2:

Presence is _____ because presence is _____.

You need to define a_____ and a _____ to come and be present with Jesus.

Read Psalm 23:

> The LORD is my shepherd, I lack nothing.
>   He makes me lie down in green pastures,
> he leads me beside quiet waters,
>   he refreshes my soul.
> He guides me along the right paths
>   for his name's sake.
> Even though I walk
>   through the darkest valley,
> I will fear no evil,
>   for you are with me;
> your rod and your staff,
>   they comfort me.
>
> You prepare a table before me
>   in the presence of my enemies.
> You anoint my head with oil;
>   my cup overflows.
> Surely your goodness and love will follow me
>   all the days of my life,
> and I will dwell in the house of the LORD
>   forever.

Write down at least five good things that happen in the company of the Lord, according to this psalm:

1.

2.

3.

4.

5.

Which of those five do you need the most right now?

The Ten Questions:
If you are with a group, discuss these for each person with the goal of that person identifying a plan to show up and spend time with Jesus.

1. What day(s) of the week can I arrange time to myself?
2. What time(s) of the day could I get at least twenty uninterrupted minutes?
3. What is the place I will be in?
4. How long can I commit to keeping this time/place?
5. What will this cost me?
6. What are common external distractions for me?
7. What can I do to deal with these ahead of time?
8. Am I willing to pray, *Help me want to come to you*?
9. Who is in my life to encourage me to keep showing up?

10. What community of believers am I committed to show-ing up in?

Make a plan and identify one person who will check in with you once a week and hold you accountable to your experiment.
Write their name here and text them if you are not together.

Pray (*together if you're in a group*) for the internal and external motivation to show up and spend time with Jesus. Tell him what you hope will happen during this time.

CHAPTER 3

Fill in the blanks from these lines in chapter 3:

In the Bible the _____ is the very core and essence of the person and, therefore, the motivator of your _____ like in Proverbs 4:23: "Above all else, guard your _____, for everything you _____ flows from it."

_____ is the only starting point with God that encourages anything real to take place.

Where does any authentic action truly begin, according to the Bible?

Read Psalm 32:

> Blessed is the one
>   whose transgressions are forgiven,
>   whose sins are covered.
> Blessed is the one
>   whose sin the LORD does not count against them
>   and in whose spirit is no deceit.
>
> When I kept silent,
>   my bones wasted away
>   through my groaning all day long.
> For day and night
>   your hand was heavy on me;
> my strength was sapped
>   as in the heat of summer.
>
> Then I acknowledged my sin to you
>   and did not cover up my iniquity.
> I said, "I will confess
>   my transgressions to the LORD."
> And you forgave
>   the guilt of my sin.
>
> Therefore let all the faithful pray to you
>   while you may be found;

surely the rising of the mighty waters
    will not reach them.
You are my hiding place;
    you will protect me from trouble
    and surround me with songs of deliverance.

I will instruct you and teach you in the way you should go;
    I will counsel you with my loving eye on you.
Do not be like the horse or the mule,
    which have no understanding
but must be controlled by bit and bridle
    or they will not come to you.
Many are the woes of the wicked,
    but the LORD's unfailing love
    surrounds the one who trusts in him.

Rejoice in the LORD and be glad, you righteous;
    sing, all you who are upright in heart!

What do you see in this psalm that encourages you to be honest with God?
If you are with a group, discuss.

What is in your heart that you'd rather avoid right now?
Tell Jesus the truth about it. Write it down here. If you are ready and able, share it with a safe group of his people.

Answer these questions to practice telling God the truth about what's in your heart:
If you are with a group, discuss.

What is my *craving*?
What do you want or need in order to live a deep, satisfied, fulfilled life?

What is my *confession*?
What truth do you need to tell yourself, others, or God that could unlock the rest of a story?

What is my *confusion*?
Are you wondering what God is doing? Has his Word left un-answered questions?

What is my *curiosity*?

Is there something you want to experience or consider a new possibility with God?

Read Psalm 139:1–12:

> You have searched me, LORD,
>   and you know me.
> You know when I sit and when I rise;
>   you perceive my thoughts from afar.
> You discern my going out and my lying down;
>   you are familiar with all my ways.
> Before a word is on my tongue
>   you, LORD, know it completely.
> You hem me in behind and before,
>   and you lay your hand upon me.
> Such knowledge is too wonderful for me,
>   too lofty for me to attain.
>
> Where can I go from your Spirit?
>   Where can I flee from your presence?
> If I go up to the heavens, you are there;
>   if I make my bed in the depths, you are there.
> If I rise on the wings of the dawn,
>   if I settle on the far side of the sea,
> even there your hand will guide me,
>   your right hand will hold me fast.
> If I say, "Surely the darkness will hide me
>   and the light become night around me,"
> even the darkness will not be dark to you;
>   the night will shine like the day,
>   for darkness is as light to you.

Pray that God would meet you in the honest space you just opened up.

CHAPTER 4

In this chapter there are three ways outlined that you can kneel down before Jesus.

If you are with a group, take time to go through each of them together, and pray for each person at the end.

▶ *1) To come to Jesus is to give up your _____.*

Where do you feel like this in your life:
"What if I trust God with my future and he really doesn't have anything good planned?"

Reflect on Proverbs 19:21:

> Many are the plans in a person's heart,
>   but it is the LORD's purpose that prevails.

Is there a plan you have been working for your life that you need to let go of?
If you are with a group, tell them.

Pray this prayer, crafted from Philippians 3:4–12, if it's time to let go of your own plan:

Lord, I am ready to stop putting confidence in my own plan and what I've been holding on to for myself. I thought I was good and strong and capable, but now I wonder if there isn't so much more I could have in you. I want to know, and I think the thing I was holding on to is now in my way of coming to you. I am willing to lose this, even though it's important to me. I know the most important thing I can do is come to you. Even if it means some sort of death, I want all the life you have for me. Amen.

► **2) To come is to give up your** _____.

Where do you feel like this in your life:
"I just keep finding new places where I'm trying it on my own and finding out I'm just not enough."

Read Ephesians 1:18–20:

> I pray that the eyes of your heart may be enlightened in order that you may know the hope to which he has called you, the riches of his glorious inheritance in his holy people, and his incomparably great power for us who believe. That power is the same as the mighty strength he exerted when he raised Christ from the dead and seated him at his right hand in the heavenly realms.

These verses tell you the source of your power for new life. Where is it?
If you are with a group, tell them.

Use this prayer, crafted from Ephesians 1:18–22, to give up on your own power and take his:

Lord, open my eyes to the hope and the future and the power I have access to in you. Help me stop believing anything else will ever be able to do what you can in my life. I want the power at work in my life to be your unique power—a power that can bring life to anyone and anything. I give up doing it with my own strength. I give up the things I was clinging to for my power or control. Come be, for me, the authority that you truly are, the one that's above every position and name and kingdom here on earth. Jesus, I see that it's you—and only you—who can be trusted with that in my life. Amen.

► **3) To come is to meet at the _____.**

Look up these verses about the cross and go deeper into its meaning in your life.

1 Corinthians 1:18: The cross looks like foolishness but it is actually what?

Ephesians 2:16: What does the cross make possible between you and God as well as you and others?

Colossians 1:20: What does the blood shed on the cross make for you?

Colossians 2:14: What got canceled and nailed to the cross?

Colossians 2:15: Who was triumphed over at the cross?

Galatians 5:11: The cross can be offensive. What do you think that means?

What is available at the cross that you most need in your life right now?

If you are with a group, tell them.

Read Romans 5:1–2:

> Therefore, since we have been justified through faith, we have peace with God through our Lord Jesus Christ, through whom we have gained access by faith into this grace in which we now stand.

When you have faith in Jesus, what are you standing on?

Physically kneel. Then pray this prayer crafted from the words of Revelation 1:17–18:

> *Jesus, I am here at your feet. Some things feel like they are dying in my life. I know I do not need to be afraid because of you. You are the first and the last. You are the living One. You were dead, and now you are alive for ever and ever. You are the key for anything in my life to come alive. I want the life you offer me at the cross. Show me how to receive your grace. Amen.*

Now stand up on grace.

HEAR: Fill in the blanks from these lines in the introduction to the practice of "Hear."

Come first. _____ second.

Hearing only leads to _____ when the Word reaches a soft, open heart.

When you come to Jesus, you receive what Jesus called "_____," which are at the heart and center of the everyday rhythms of come, hear, practice.

Use your favorite translation and write out Isaiah 40:8 here.

Is there an instance that you remember hearing God somehow? What was that like? How did you know? If you remember the words you heard, write them down here.
If you are with a group, share these stories out loud.

CHAPTER 5

Describe a "tipping point" in your own words.
If you are with a group, describe what it looks like in your life when you are overwhelmed with words and just check out.

Fill in the blanks from chapter 5:

A strong _____ for your life requires regular, authentic exchanges between you and your Father through the _____.

When your _____ ears get a break from the words, your _____ ears start to work better. It gives margin for the voice of God in your day.

Make a list here of the decisions—small, medium, and large—you are facing right now:
If you are with a group, share out loud which one(s) currently spin around most in your mind.

1.

2.

3.

4.

5.

How comfortable are you with silence?

__ Very. Love it, actually.

__ I'm fine either way.

__ I guess I can do it but don't usually.

__ I prefer music or something on most of the time.

__ Something feels off when it's too quiet.

What are some possible times during your day or week that you could be in silence? Brainstorm at least five ideas.
If you are with a group, share ideas to help each other be creative.

1.

2.

3.

4.

5.

Make a list of the top ten things you feel you *should* be doing in your life. Some are right. Some need to be questioned. But most of these you likely can't imagine *not* doing!

1.

2.

3.

4.

5.

6.

7.

8.

9.

10.

Is there one "should" you could experiment with setting aside for quiet or for time with Jesus this week?
If you are with a group, ask them if you chose the right one. Others see more clearly where you're under the influence of an unnecessary "should."

Read Matthew 11:28–30 (MSG):

Are you tired? Worn out? Burned out on religion? Come to me. Get away with me and you'll recover your life. I'll show you how to take a real rest. Walk with me and work with me—watch how I do it. Learn the unforced rhythms of grace. I won't lay anything heavy or ill-fitting on you. Keep company with me and you'll learn to live freely and lightly.

How did those verses make you feel? Which specific words do you spark to the most?
If you are with a group, go around and say the words out loud. See which are in common.

What's the question in this chapter that you need to ask of all the words you hear?

How does this chapter suggest you'll know if words are going to bring you life?

Read 2 Kings 22. What does Josiah do when he realizes God's Word was not being heard among the people? What happens to him as a result?

Look up John 6:63 in your favorite translation and write it here.

CHAPTER 6

Fill in the blanks from chapter 6:

Your job? Have a _____. Run it faithfully. And stay near him. You have to be able to hear his _____.

_____ is the secret to a thriving connection to God. A plan might not sound fun or sexy or even particularly spiritual, but it's critical to you getting to know the

_____.

The Word is alive in us if we have the _____. It is accessible to us even when we aren't sitting with a Bible in our hand, working our reading plan. But hearing his voice regularly starts right there, with reading and listening to his Word.

In this chapter, a brief plan is given for spending time with God. You're going to practice doing that right now!

PRAISE: Spend at least five minutes writing down praise for who God is.

- For inspiration, read any of the following or find your own: Genesis 1; Exodus 34:5–7; Psalm 18:1–2; Psalm 86:5–10; Psalm 89; Isaiah 40:27–29; John 8:12; John 15:1–17; Revelation 21:1–8. *If you are with a group, choose several and read out loud together.*

READ: **Read a paragraph of Scripture from the plan you are following or the plan on page 95.**
In a group, it will be best to read the same passage. Decide now what that is before going further.

- What piece of Scripture are you reading right now?

  _____

- **Observe.** What do you see or notice about the actual text and words of this passage? No application here. Just make good observations like the following: The verb "were justified" is past tense; Jesus called himself by another name, Son of Man; the context of this interaction was a festival in Jerusalem. *With a group, make a big list on a whiteboard or paper so all can see.*

- **Summarize.** Put the main idea in your own words here:

- **Interact.** Tell God whatever you want about this reading. Ask questions. Express emotion. You aren't deciding on meaning; you're just personally relating. *Discuss out loud in a group.*

- **Connect.** Take a few minutes to connect this reading to whatever comes right before it. How are they connected?

- **Anchor.** Identify the one verse or phrase that you want to take with you. Write it here five to seven times. *If you're with a group, share out loud what each person chose from the reading.*

PRAY: **Pray for God's will and kingdom, provision, forgiveness, help, or rescue in any aspect of life for**

1. Yourself
2. Your friends, people, and/or leaders
3. Your church
4. Your community/city
5. Your country and world

Experiment with an add-on to the praise, read, pray basic meeting plan.

- Reread what each of these are on pages 99–101 and choose what goes best with the time, Scripture, mind, and heart you have this week.

- Circle the one you plan to do. Then do it. *If you're with a group, share your choice, discuss the experience, or teach what you learned.*

Deeper study	Audio	Memorize Scripture
Follow-up notes	Brain dump	Read a devotional
Silence	Music	Surround yourself

Good work. I hope you feel more equipped to spend time with Jesus!

CHAPTER 7

Fill in the blanks from chapter 7:
The Holy Spirit is going to draw you into a brand-new
_____.

With _____ books, _____ authors, and written over _____ years, Scripture actually does tell one story.

Whatever story _____ wrote for your own life might just be what's preventing you from hearing the voice of _____.

As you learn his past through the Scriptures, you'll *know* him better, so you'll be able to tune your _____ to his _____.

The Bible is actually your story, and _____ is your way in.

In chapter 7, I gave an example of one part of the story of Scripture that is meaningful to our own stories in God's

family. Let's go on another hunt through Scripture to practice seeing and learning another part of your story. Although I am giving you the Scripture references, this is an example of what *you* might pick up on as you read through the Bible. Seeing, understanding, and interpreting the unfolding story of your own life through the lens of Scripture can help you practice living in the kingdom of God right here and now.

Another part of your story: *the wilderness.* When you are in periods of time you'd characterize as a wilderness season, God is still at work. But that work is often misunderstood. Knowing wilderness is part of God's story as well can help you accept, pray, process, and lean into it in your life. Instead of swallowing the story the world gives you about what to do here and how to deal with it, knowing God's story could reframe questions like, What is God doing? Is it always the same? Am I going to come out? Knowing the story of God in Scripture can help you live through it in your own life today.

If you are with a group, look up, read, and discuss the following passages. Or split them up for homework and discuss the next time you meet.

Read Genesis 3 (especially vv. 21–24). What happened to put Adam and Eve into a wilderness?

Read Exodus 3:1–10. What happened to Moses in the wilderness?

Read Exodus 16. What did the Israelites complain about in the wilderness, and how did God respond?

Read Joshua 5:4–6 and Psalm 106:24–27. Why did God say that an entire generation of Israel died in the wilderness?

Read Nehemiah 9:19–20. How does Nehemiah characterize God's dealings with Israel in the wilderness?

Read 1 Samuel 23:14. What was the role of the wilderness in David's life at this point in time?

Read Jeremiah 31:1–2. What was the role of the wilderness here, according to Jeremiah?

Read John 1:22–23. What did John the Baptist say happens in the wilderness?

Read Matthew 3:13–17. Why do you think the wilderness was the next thing that happened?

Read Matthew 4:1. Who led Jesus into the wilderness?

Read Matthew 4:1–11. What temptations are in the wilderness?

After reading all the passages noted here about the wilderness, what are some possible ways that God has used or is using the wilderness in your life and story? How does it connect to Jesus?
If you are with a group, discuss.

PRACTICE: Fill in the blanks from these lines in the introduction to "Practice."

Practicing isn't simply about _____; it's about _____.

_____ the evidence that the first two rhythms genuinely took root.

Finishing these three rhythms in succession—_____, _____, _____—will not only form rock at the foundation of your life but you'll experience the joy and adventure of getting to know a living God.

What is the problem we get ourselves into when it's summertime and there's hard, packed sand? Write it in your own words.
If you are with a group, compare your responses with each other.

Read Hebrews 4:12. What does it say about the Word of God?
(*Hint: both words begin with "a"!*)

When is the last time you remember being obedient to God or to his Word? What did you do?
If you are with a group, share these stories out loud.

CHAPTER 8

Fill in the blanks from chapter 8:
Living a life of faith doesn't mean an absence of _____ or _____; it just means you practice anyway. You practice when you're not _____.

There's a _____ that comes when you practice the Word of God.

Practice really is a _____, so we can't wait for the whole _____ to be revealed.

What is the question in this chapter that you need to ask about any area of your life to find a good chance to practice?

Read Hebrews 11:6. What does this verse say pleases God?

Read Romans 5:2. What does this verse say we are standing in? Why would you need that to practice?

Where in your life are you *waiting to be more certain* of what God wants you to do? What would practicing faith look like in this place?
If you are with a group, discuss.

If you find yourself waiting on perfect information or certainty before you move, memorize Psalm 23:3–4:

He guides me along the right paths
    for his name's sake.
Even though I walk
    through the darkest valley,
I will fear no evil,
    for you are with me.

Where in your life are you *waiting for the full picture* to be revealed? What would practicing faith look like in this place?
If you are with a group, discuss.

If you find yourself wanting the full picture before you move, memorize Proverbs 3:5–6 this week:

Trust in the Lord with all your heart
    and lean not on your own understanding;
in all your ways submit to him,
    and he will make your paths straight.

Where in your life are you *waiting to get stronger* before you move? What would practicing faith look like in this place? *If you are with a group, discuss.*

If you feel too weak to move, memorize 2 Corinthians 12:9 this week:

But he said to me, "My grace is sufficient for you, for my power is made perfect in weakness." Therefore I will boast all the more gladly about my weaknesses, so that Christ's power may rest on me.

CHAPTER 9

Fill in the blanks from chapter 9:
_____ is a part of practice.

There is opposition to the words of God because there is an _____ of God.

The presence of the _____ is what actually introduces the conflict in practicing God's Word.

Be aware of the resistance that's coming for you so that you don't miss the _____.

Practice is the moment your _____ gets stronger, but resistance is designed to stop that.

In Scripture, God often tests people's commitment to the _____ and _____ of his kingdom.

As the Spirit invites you to practice, you are *not* going to ask him _____ before you move.

The enemy of God puts up resistance to your practice of the Word in three ways. Write down the three phrases of resistance here that are outlined in the chapter:

1.

2.

3.

Do you have an internal struggle going on right now? Put both sides of the tug-of-war into your own words.
If you are with a group, share these out loud.

After reading chapter 9, what kind of resistance is closest to what you have experienced in that struggle?
If you are with a group, make a tally of the type of resistance you're all going through so you can encourage one another in it.

Have you ever experienced what you believe was a test of faith? Why does this stand out as a test?
If you are with a group, share these out loud.

What are the things you're asking God for more of in your life? Consider and reflect here about whether there could be a test in front of you right now.

Read Matthew 20:20–28 about asking for more and the test that comes with it. Answer the questions below from the passage.

> Then the mother of Zebedee's sons came to Jesus with her sons and, kneeling down, asked a favor of him.
>
> "What is it you want?" he asked.
>
> She said, "Grant that one of these two sons of mine may sit at your right and the other at your left in your kingdom."
>
> "You don't know what you are asking," Jesus said to them. "Can you drink the cup I am going to drink?"
>
> "We can," they answered.
>
> Jesus said to them, "You will indeed drink from my cup, but to sit at my right or left is not for me to grant. These places belong to those for whom they have been prepared by my Father."
>
> When the ten heard about this, they were indignant with the two brothers. Jesus called them together and said, "You know that the rulers of the Gentiles lord it over them, and their high officials exercise authority over them. Not so with you. Instead, whoever wants to become great among you must be your servant, and whoever wants to be first must be your slave—just as the Son of Man did not come to be served, but to serve, and to give his life as a ransom for many."

What more did this mother want for her sons?

What was the test that Jesus said would come for anyone who wants more power?

Pray this prayer:

Father, help me to see where you are preparing me for more. Help me push through resistance to practice your Word. I'd specifically like help with this temptation or struggle or test or resistance right now in my life. Amen.

CHAPTER 10

Fill in the blanks from chapter 10:
The Holy Spirit will help you stay _____ to Jesus in a real relationship.

The Spirit is a _____—not a spiritual force. Discovering and developing a deeper connection with him through practice of the Word is the very essence of having a relationship with Jesus.

God likes who he made and expects you to be _____.

Your signature move is one of three actions. List those here:

1.

2.

3.

Which of these descriptions sounds most like what could be *your* signature move? Why?
If you are with a group, share your signature moves and discuss.

List three positive change-points you've experienced in your life. Write down what you did. What, specifically, did you do that contributed to the shift in trajectory? Do you see any similarities in these instances? If so, what?
If you are with a group, discuss.

Change-points:

1.

2.

3.

Reflect here:

Do you think your signature move is *obey*? Memorize this verse this week:

> By faith Abraham, when called to go to a place he would later receive as his inheritance, obeyed and went, even though he did not know where he was going. (Heb. 11:8)

Do you think your signature move is *receive*? Memorize this verse this week:

> Now you, brothers and sisters, like Isaac, are children of promise. (Gal. 4:28)

Do you think your signature move is *hustle*? Memorize this verse this week:

> Your name will no longer be Jacob, but Israel, because you have struggled with God and with humans and have overcome. (Gen. 32:28)

Read Rahab's story in Joshua 2:1–16 as Israel was moving toward the promised land.

> Then Joshua son of Nun secretly sent two spies from Shittim. "Go, look over the land," he said, "especially Jericho." So they went and entered the house of a prostitute named Rahab and stayed there.
>
> The king of Jericho was told, "Look, some of the Israelites have come here tonight to spy out the land." So the king of Jericho sent this message to Rahab: "Bring out the men who came to you and entered your house, because they have come to spy out the whole land."
>
> But the woman had taken the two men and hidden them. She said, "Yes, the men came to me, but I did not know where they had come from. At dusk, when it was time to close the city gate, they left. I don't know which way they went. Go after them

quickly. You may catch up with them." (But she had taken them up to the roof and hidden them under the stalks of flax she had laid out on the roof.) So the men set out in pursuit of the spies on the road that leads to the fords of the Jordan, and as soon as the pursuers had gone out, the gate was shut.

Before the spies lay down for the night, she went up on the roof and said to them, "I know that the LORD has given you this land and that a great fear of you has fallen on us, so that all who live in this country are melting in fear because of you. We have heard how the LORD dried up the water of the Red Sea for you when you came out of Egypt, and what you did to Sihon and Og, the two kings of the Amorites east of the Jordan, whom you completely destroyed. When we heard of it, our hearts melted in fear and everyone's courage failed because of you, for the LORD your God is God in heaven above and on the earth below.

"Now then, please swear to me by the LORD that you will show kindness to my family, because I have shown kindness to you. Give me a sure sign that you will spare the lives of my father and mother, my brothers and sisters, and all who belong to them—and that you will save us from death."

"Our lives for your lives!" the men assured her. "If you don't tell what we are doing, we will treat you kindly and faithfully when the LORD gives us the land."

So she let them down by a rope through the window, for the house she lived in was part of the city wall. She said to them, "Go to the hills so the pursuers will not find you. Hide yourselves there three days until they return, and then go on your way."

God dealt with Rahab right where she was. What surprised you about her or this story?

What signature move do you think Rahab put on display: *obey*, *receive*, or *hustle*?

CHAPTER 11

Fill in the blanks from chapter 11:

_____ is an essential part of living out the three rhythms of *coming* to Jesus, *hearing* his Word, and putting it into *practice*. It's going to lead you straight into a risk.

Risk isn't a personality trait; it's a _____ you can learn, strengthen, and grow.

The risks you take on _____ are the ones that will turn your foundation to rock.

Risk is the path on which you move toward _____. It's the way you get to the well-built life you want.

As you risk, your _____ to risk grows, and your relationship with Jesus gets more solid.

You don't have to think of yourself as a risk-taker to become one; you just have to want to _____.

Do you think of yourself as a risk-taker?

__ Yes
__ No

What is the last risk you remember taking on in your life? How did you feel about it?
If you are with a group, share these out loud.

Rewrite Matthew 17:20 here from your favorite translation:

Write three to five words describing the amount, type, and nature of your trust for God at this point in your life.

Do you see a risk you think *God* may want you to take right now? If so, what is it?
If you are with a group or alone, pray for the Spirit to bring to mind any risk God is asking you to take.

What doubts do you have about this risk right now?
Say these out loud to someone and let them respond.

What is the outcome you are hoping for? How is this impacting your willingness and doubt?

Say this prayer to God where relevant in your life right now: "I do believe; help me overcome my unbelief!" (Mark 9:24).

Look up Hebrews 11:1 and rewrite it in your own words.

What were the words of Jesus that he often issued as an invitation to take a risk? (*Hint: it's on page 162.*)

One last chapter 11 fill-in-the-blank!

God knows the places of unbelief in you, and he's going to offer you a _____ _____ _____ that will prove he is enough in that very spot.

CHAPTER 12

Fill in the blanks from chapter 12:
The _____ is already part of your rebuilding. God is at work in the _____.

The very things that have your life in pieces can be the beginning of _____ forming under your feet again.

There is nothing God cannot _____.

Some parts of our lives are being held up by _____.

Rebuilding is possible because of the foundational work of Jesus on the _____.

He is the ultimate _____, the ultimate _____, the unbreakable _____.

Is there a part of your life that has partially or completely fallen apart? Reread this sinkhole prayer and then write your own to God below it.

> Rescue me from the mire,
>   do not let me sink;
> deliver me from those who hate me,
>   from the deep waters.
> Do not let the floodwaters engulf me
>   or the depths swallow me up
>   or the pit close its mouth over me.
>   (Ps. 69:14–15)

Your sinkhole prayer:

Look up Psalm 34:18 in your favorite translation and rewrite it here.

What part of your life hasn't yet fallen down, but right now you feel the ground shifting?
If you're in a group, share these and have someone pray for courage for all to get to solid ground, beginning with truly coming to God in this place.

Read Psalm 51. This is a psalm of David after he committed adultery with Bathsheba (after which he had her husband killed)—not his finest moment. Reflect below.

> Have mercy on me, O God,
>   according to your unfailing love;
> according to your great compassion
>   blot out my transgressions.
> Wash away all my iniquity
>   and cleanse me from my sin.
>
> For I know my transgressions,
>   and my sin is always before me.

Against you, you only, have I sinned
    and done what is evil in your sight;
so you are right in your verdict
    and justified when you judge.
Surely I was sinful at birth,
    sinful from the time my mother conceived me.
Yet you desired faithfulness even in the womb;
    you taught me wisdom in that secret place.

Cleanse me with hyssop, and I will be clean;
    wash me, and I will be whiter than snow.
Let me hear joy and gladness;
    let the bones you have crushed rejoice.
Hide your face from my sins
    and blot out all my iniquity.

Create in me a pure heart, O God,
    and renew a steadfast spirit within me.
Do not cast me from your presence
    or take your Holy Spirit from me.
Restore to me the joy of your salvation
    and grant me a willing spirit, to sustain me.

Then I will teach transgressors your ways,
    so that sinners will turn back to you.
Deliver me from the guilt of bloodshed, O God,
    you who are God my Savior,
    and my tongue will sing of your righteousness.
Open my lips, Lord,
    and my mouth will declare your praise.
You do not delight in sacrifice, or I would bring it;
    you do not take pleasure in burnt offerings.
My sacrifice, O God, is a broken spirit;
    a broken and contrite heart
    you, God, will not despise.

May it please you to prosper Zion,
    to build up the walls of Jerusalem.

Then you will delight in the sacrifices of the righteous,
in burnt offerings offered whole;
then bulls will be offered on your altar.

Reflect on these verses:

- Read verse 1: What qualities of God does David call on in a part of his life that is crumbling?
- Read verses 2 and 7: What verbs does David use? What does he ask God to do?
- Read verses 3–5: David is coming to God with a confession. If you have one, write it below.
- Read verses 10–12: What verbs does David use here? What is he asking for?
- Read verse 13: What does David believe his story will do to help others? Yours can do the same.
- Read verse 17: What reassurance does this verse give you?

Reflect here.

Close your eyes and imagine yourself new. Your life standing on rock. All the right parts and relationships rebuilt. Your connection with God strong. What and who is there? What and who isn't? How do you feel? What does it look like? What

colors and images do you imagine? Write down here what you picture.

If you are with a group, take turns describing what you pictured.

Grace means it's never too late to rebuild. It's always a good time to come, hear, and practice a life of real faith. What grace do you need from God to start that right now? Write it here.

If you are with a group, share it out loud.

Read verses 1–5 from both Revelation 21 and 22. This is the end of the biblical story and of your story in Christ. Circle one phrase you love that makes you want to *come* to Jesus, *hear* his words, and put them into *practice*.

Revelation 21:1–5

> Then I saw "a new heaven and a new earth," for the first heaven and the first earth had passed away, and there was no longer any sea. I saw the Holy City, the new Jerusalem, coming down out of heaven from God, prepared as a bride beautifully dressed for her husband. And I heard a loud voice from the throne saying, "Look! God's dwelling place is now among the people, and he will dwell with them. They will be his people, and God himself will be with them and be their God. 'He will wipe every tear from their eyes. There will be no more death' or mourning or crying or pain, for the old order of things has passed away."
>
> He who was seated on the throne said, "I am making everything new!" Then he said, "Write this down, for these words are trustworthy and true."

Revelation 22:1–5

> Then the angel showed me the river of the water of life, as clear as crystal, flowing from the throne of God and of the Lamb down the middle of the great street of the city. On each side of the river stood the tree of life, bearing twelve crops of fruit, yielding its fruit every month. And the leaves of the tree are for the healing of the nations. No longer will there be any curse. The throne of God and of the Lamb will be in the city, and his servants will serve him. They will see his face, and his name will be on their foreheads. There will be no more night. They will not need the light of a lamp or the light of the sun, for the Lord God will give them light. And they will reign for ever and ever.

Alli Patterson is passionate about helping others build a life on the firm foundation of Jesus, connected to God through his Word. She holds a master's degree in biblical studies from Dallas Theological Seminary and is a teaching pastor at Crossroads Church. She lives in Cincinnati, Ohio, with her husband, Bill, their four children, and one very bratty cat. Learn more at theallipatterson.com.

Want to learn more from Alli Patterson? Visit her online at

TheAlliPatterson.com

for access to Scripture-based Bible studies, podcasts, book

recommendations, teaching videos, and more!